T0167079

FINDING AESCULAPIUS ACROSS THE ATLANTIC

The Road to Discovery

A Memoir

NICHOLAS A. KEFALIDES

iUniverse, Inc.
Bloomington

Finding Aesculapius across the Atlantic
The Road to Discovery

Copyright © 2012 Nicholas A. Kefalides

All rights reserved. No part of this book may be used or reproduced by any means, graphic, electronic, or mechanical, including photocopying, recording, taping or by any information storage retrieval system without the written permission of the publisher except in the case of brief quotations embodied in critical articles and reviews.

iUniverse books may be ordered through booksellers or by contacting:

iUniverse
1663 Liberty Drive
Bloomington, IN 47403
www.iuniverse.com
1-800-Authors (1-800-288-4677)

Because of the dynamic nature of the Internet, any Web addresses or links contained in this book may have changed since publication and may no longer be valid. The views expressed in this work are solely those of the author and do not necessarily reflect the views of the publisher, and the publisher hereby disclaims any responsibility for them.

Any people depicted in stock imagery provided by Thinkstock are models, and such images are being used for illustrative purposes only.

Certain stock imagery © Thinkstock.

ISBN: 978-1-4759-1397-2 (sc)
ISBN: 978-1-4759-1398-9 (e)

Printed in the United States of America

iUniverse rev. date: 05/04/2012

TABLE OF CONTENTS

DEDICATION

THIS BOOK IS DEDICATED to the memory of my parents, Athanasios and Alexandra, to Uncle John and Aunt Bettie and to the memory of Sanford M. Rosenthal and Augusto Bazan and the many physicians and staff of the Peru Burn Project.

My thanks go to my wife Jane, my son Paul and my daughter Patricia Theodosopoulos for their enormous help with the editing of the book.

*Aesculapius is the god of medicine and healing
in ancient Greek religion. He and his daughters,
Hygieia (Hygiene), Iaso (Medicine), Aceso (Healing),
Aglaea (Healthy Glow) and Panacea (Universal
Remedy), complete the pantheon of medicine.*

PROLOGUE

IN MY FIRST MEMOIR *"Echoes From The Cobblestones,"* I described my experiences from the first two decades of my life in Greece, during the 1930's and 1940's. The most trying years of that period were from 1940 to 1944, the years of war and of German occupation. The current memoir has as its target a broad audience, which includes family members, friends, medical colleagues and scientists at large.

It was October 28, 1944 when the German army was forced to abandon Thessaloniki, Greece, where my family and I lived during the years of the Second World War. Soon the Germans were departing from the whole of Greece as the allied forces were pounding them in western and southern Europe and on the Russian front.

In the intervening years between October 1944 and May 1947, my parents and Aunt Helen and I began to think seriously about my going to America.

My high school classmates and I graduated from the Peiramatikon Scholeion (Experimental School) of the Aristotelion University of Thessaloniki in December 1945. Seven of the seventeen who graduated in 1945, took the entrance exam and were admitted to the School of Medicine. Our group attended classes for only two and a half months, from May 1946 to the middle of July 1946. That short period of classes in the spring of 1946 was wiped out and we were asked to begin our first year of medical school classes anew in the fall, along with those students who graduated from high school in July 1946.

The opening in 1946 of the sea-lanes for commercial travel between Europe and the United States led to an exodus of young men and women from England and from formerly occupied countries of Europe who began to emigrate to America. This was an unprecedented phenomenon. Some of these young people were U.S. citizens who along with their families were caught in Europe after the U.S. entered the Second World War and were now being repatriated. The majority, however, were new emigrants who did not arrive as refugees or as individuals seeking political asylum. They were people who sought to pursue specific aims— to work in an uncle's business or to pursue studies in universities, such as medical specialties, engineering, physics, chemistry and biology.

My turn to immigrate to the U.S.A. as a student finally arrived in late 1946, when Uncle John, my father's brother, sent the necessary documents for obtaining an American Visa. I had moved to Athens at the beginning of April of 1947 to begin gathering the papers necessary for obtaining a Greek passport and a Visa.

When I confronted the process of obtaining a visa, the many steps loomed like an untenable challenge. It soon became evident that I had to negotiate through a Greek bureaucratic maze. My Uncle Nick, who was married to a cousin of my father's and my Uncle Elias, my father's brother, both lawyers, knew the necessary contacts in Athens and helped with the whole procedure.

In the middle of April 1947 I visited Thessaloniki to say goodbye to my parents, my brother Chris, my grandparents, and all the relatives and friends.

My Greek passport was issued on April 26, 1947 and was handed to the U.S. Consular Clerk a few days before my departure, which was scheduled for May 5, 1947, so that the U.S. Consul could attach the Visa.

On the afternoon of May 5, 1947 Uncle Elias and Uncle Nick took me down to the port of Piraeus where I boarded my temporary home for the next two weeks, the Italian liner "Saturnia". The transatlantic voyage began on a warm afternoon, as the sun was slowly hiding behind the mountain ranges of Olympus and Ossa, casting a shimmering glow on the calm sea. We made only one stop and that was in Naples to pick up Italian emmigrants. On May 19, 1947 we arrived in New York harbor. Because of the late afternoon arrival we were asked to stay overnight in our cabins until the next morning when the immigration authorities came aboard and checked our visas and passports. Following the passport control we went through customs.

The ten days I spent in Astoria, Long Island, as a guest of Uncle George, my father's older brother, his wife Aunt Katina and their son, Nick, were a very pleasant and rewarding experience. Seeing the awesome skyscrapers in Manhattan, evoked the same initial impressions I had experienced as a young boy of 11 in 1938 when I arrived in Thessaloniki and was treated to those beautiful high-rise buildings.

On May 29, 1947 I arrived in Chicago, where Uncle John met me at the train station. We took the subway to Evanston, Illinois the first suburb north of Chicago, where Uncle John and Aunt Bettie lived. I was given my own room with a queen size bed, beautiful floral wallpaper, my own closet and my own desk with a glass top—one of Uncle John's earlier desks. I slowly began to develop a new sense of individuality, a person whose needs and requirements were recognized by Uncle John.

My arrival in Evanston, Illinois, on May 29, 1947, signaled a new life for me; a life that was characterized by an array of events that, although at the time I did not perceive them as challenges, they represented obstacles that had to be overcome.

My first and most obvious challenge was learning English. Uncle John decided that learning the new language from a book entitled "English

Self Taught" would be both easy and inexpensive. And that's how it went.

Three months after arriving in Evanston, I had to start college. The first language problem I faced was the need to take a multiple choice entrance exam in college, not to determine admittance, but to use the performance on the test as a baseline to compare it with subsequent progress. Needless to say I had not taken a multiple-choice test before. In addition, I requested the use of an English-Greek dictionary, which I was allowed to do.

After completing four years of college and university studies, I began investigating the entrance requirements for medical school and realized that it was not an easy process, especially at a state school like the University of Illinois. Not being a permanent resident was a serious but not an absolute impediment. It was, however, another serious challenge. In 1951, I decided to enter the graduate school of the University of Illinois in Champagne-Urbana, while my second application to the School of Medicine was pending. My performance and my grades in the graduate school convinced the medical school admissions committee to accept me. In addition to helping my application to medical school, the graduate school work was intrinsically valuable; the experiences with microbial genetics, virology and biochemistry had a profound effect on my future medical career. In the early spring of 1952 I received an acceptance letter from the University of Illinois College of Medicine.

The four years of medical school were another challenging experience, which I successfully overcame. My performance was such that I was given a student NIH research grant to pursue research in my spare time. My research led to a master's degree in biochemistry, which was awarded on the same day as my M.D. in 1956.

The experience that tops all so far and I consider the epitome of a challenging task, was the request by my mentors to join the NIH and move with my wife to Lima, Peru, to direct a government project on the prevention and treatment of shock and infections in skin burns. It is easy to see why I place this challenge so high on the list. At the time of this transition, I was just finishing my internship, I had no experience with burns or clinical trials and I spoke no Spanish.

What I realize now is that my mentors had a great deal of confidence and trust in my then untested ability to carry out such duties in a strange land. My diligence proved them right..

After the Lima, Peru, experience, I returned to Chicago and was a happy resident in Internal Medicine, taking care of my patients and teaching my interns. At the end of two years I was given my certificate for successfully fulfilling the training requirements. This now allowed me to start a two-year fellowship in Infectious Diseases.

Soon, I was named Chief of the trainees in Infectious Diseases and was at the same time appointed as Junior Attending Physician at Cook County Hospital.

Suddenly, my mentors found a new way to perturb my academic tranquility with a suggestion that I enroll in the graduate school of the University of Illinois and work for an advanced degree, a Ph.D., in Biochemistry. Although this was as demanding a challenge as any I had encountered so far, my reservations were countered by my professors who pointed out that I was going to receive a large annual stipend of about $9500.00, almost three times as much as my Fellowship salary and that the Ph.D. would help advance my academic career. In the fall of 1962, I began my research project whose goal was to identify the antigenic components of the kidney glomerular basement membranes.

As this memoir unfolds, it becomes evident that the previous challenges paved the way to a successful academic career, which culminated in my becoming a *bona fide* faculty member in three universities and in pursuing a research program replete with discoveries.

Such is the patriot's boast, where'er we roam,
his first, best country ever, is at Home.
Oliver Goldsmith, *The Traveler, 1764*

CHAPTER 1

Crossing The Atlantic

IN THE FINAL THREE weeks before I said goodbye to my family, friends and the whole of Greece, I had to take care of what seemed like a myriad of things.

As a student of the School of Medicine at the Aristotelion University of Thessaloniki, I had to get the signatures of the head professors (chairmen) of the various departments in my book of studies, attesting to the fact that I was a pupil in good standing. Since I did not know what the future held for me and whether I would be staying permanently in the USA or returning to Greece at sometime in the future to resume my university studies, the signatures were important and necessary.

On a bright, sunny day I arrived at the university and went straight to the office of Professor Kavasiades, chairman of the chemistry department. I was first met by an older individual, the professor's clerk, who asked me to state my business. I indicated that I needed the Professor's signature and without saying a word, he entered the professor's office and within

1

a few minutes he returned and let me in to see Professor Kavasiades. The duration of my stay in Mr. Kavasiades office was barely a moment longer than it took for me to address him and say "Kyrie Kavasiade" (Mister Kavasiades). Mr. Kavasiades told me in an angry tone to get out of his office and not to return until I learned how to address a professor. Reprimanded, I walked out and again was met by the clerk, who whispered in a reassuring tone, "Leave the book with me and come back tomorrow. I will put it on his desk and he will sign it along with a few others." The next morning I visited the professor's office and the old man handed me the book all properly signed. Apparently, Mr. Kavasiades wanted to be addressed as " Mr. Professor. It was comparatively easy to get three more signatures from the professors of zoology, anatomy and gymnastics—then I was ready to travel.

As the day of my departure from Thessaloniki was approaching, my parents took advantage of every opportunity to sit down with me and talk about the upcoming, long voyage across the Atlantic. They could not completely ignore the potential hazards of such a long trip, be they stormy seas or a stray sea mine, a World War II remnant. I had to assuage their fears first by indicating that the liner was seaworthy and safe and that it had completed the same voyage several times before without any problems. The issue with the floating mines was not as easy to dismiss. My parents had read too many newspaper stories and seen enough war movies to make them apprehensive about the mines, especially when they are invisible at night. Again I had to point out that in the two years since the war ended the allied countries had spared no effort to seek and destroy the mines.

My parents acted like all parents, making sure I was aware that I was moving into a country with different ways of life and customs. Despite the fact that my new guardians were going to be Uncle John and Aunt Bettie, my folks wanted to emphasize the importance of obeying Uncle John and Aunt Bettie and not acting like a sassy person.

I was leaving Thessaloniki for Athens amid a throng of family members and relatives who had gathered at the port of the city to see me off. I received hugs and kisses in a repetitive fashion. The Greek expression *kalo taxidi* (have a good trip) was the phrase I was hearing as I was walking toward the ship. Before I walked up the gangway I hugged and kissed my father and then my mother, as she was wiping the tears running down her cheeks.

The desire to study medicine or specialize abroad was not an uncommon practice for those whose families could arrange it and afford it. Some of my classmates who chose to study medicine followed different paths. George Kostopoulos, the son of a surgeon, was ready to travel to Geneva, Switzerland to attend medical school at the University of Geneva. For several years George was studying French at home under the tutelage of a very capable French teacher, so when he arrived in Geneva, he was speaking French fluently. He finished his medical studies in six years but soon after he had to return to Thessaloniki because his father died and he was expected to take over the management of the clinic that his father established a few years back. The remaining five classmates, who entered medical school, finished their studies and either stayed in Greece or travelled abroad to pursue studies in different specialties. Tasos Oikonomou, Ioulios Iossifides and Angelos Kalogeropoulos travelled to the USA, the first two to pursue pathology and the third cardiology. Alekos Andreadis went to England to specialize in neurosurgery. The one who stayed in Greece after graduation from medical school, Mimis Kazakides, became a clinical microbiologist.

The day that I was to be given my American visa arrived and I was asked to go to the consular office for an interview with the American Consul General. I entered his room and was greeted by a smiling, tall, blond, young man who asked me to take a seat. Looking at this young, handsome, man I felt the anxiety, which had been building up for the past few days, begin to dissipate.

He opened my file, read it and asked me, with the smile never leaving his face, "Why do you want to go to America?" and I replied in the simplest English I could master "To study medicine." He closed the file, stood up, and extending his hand said "Congratulations and good luck."

While waiting for all the paperwork to be finalized, I was fortunate to meet Vangelis Mikronmastoras, a friend from Thessaloniki, who was attending the University of Athens. Another friend and his sister, Frangiskos and Louisa Samaritas, from Thessaloniki were also in Athens. At this time of the year we had unusually pleasant weather in Athens, with clear skies and temperatures around 74 degrees F, (about 24 degrees Celsius). The four of us met frequently and enjoyed going on walks in the parks of Athens or on picnics. We chose our picnic sites carefully, preferring hilly areas covered with pine trees along an isolated beach. Meeting with friends from Thessaloniki tended to soften the concerns and sadness of leaving the places I grew up with in Greece—the places that gave me memorable, pleasant and unforgettable experiences. The topic of conversation almost invariably centered on the future of Greece and on our plans for university studies. I explained that my immediate goal had been determined; I was planning to go to medical school when I got to the United States. I had no idea then that the system in the U.S. required a four-year pre-medical study program before applying for medical school at the end of the third year.

Vangelis Micromastoras was pursuing a career in chemistry at the University of Athens, whereas Frangiskos and his sister Louisa did not continue further studies after graduating from high school.

On the morning of the day of departure from the port of Piraeus, I was walking near Omonia Square and I noticed a movie theater featuring a movie with Basil Rathbone. I immediately reasoned that for two weeks on the ship I will probably not have a chance to see a movie and quickly bought a ticket. I enjoyed the picture. It showed Basil Rathbone uncovering and chasing Nazi spies in America. Meanwhile, Uncles Elias and Nick were looking for me and since I had not left word with the hotel desk where I was going, my uncles became concerned and panicky. When

I walked into the hotel at noon, they were very relieved to see that I was O.K. and they forgot the incident.

At 5 P.M. on May 5, 1947, I said goodbye to Uncles Elias and Nick and I boarded the liner "Saturnia". I was shown my bunk in the first tier below deck and as soon as I put my head on the pillow I fell fast asleep. About an hour later we were informed that dinner was served. The staple item in the menu was spaghetti and meat sauce, which was quite tasty and filling. At dinnertime I had the opportunity to meet other Greek passengers as well as some from Egypt. After dinner we moved to the dance hall where we sat at the available tables. The conversations centered on our future plans when we arrive in America. Despite the fact that the majority of the passengers were Greek, Italian, Egyptian and others of unknown nationality, we managed to find ways to communicate primarily in our broken English and not infrequently using sign language. However, attention was given more to the tune played by the orchestra and the dance steps than to the topics of conversation. We shared our hopes for success as well as our fears of failure and uncertainties about what lay ahead for us in America. Despite all the talk of possible success or failure we managed to meet two to three times a week in the Saturnia's big hall and danced to the tunes of popular Italian and Greek music.

On the afternoon of May 18, we arrived in the port of New York and the prevailing mood quickly changed from gloom to glee . The captain informed us that we were not going to disembark that evening due to the late hour but we would be doing so the next morning after going through immigration control.

In only a few moments after dropping anchor in New York that first evening, there were spontaneous groups of young passengers congregating on the main deck, then descending to the main hall where the dancing, drinking and singing celebration took place.

On the morning of May 19, 1947 we began to disembark. I presented my file to an immigration official who after going through it, gave me a green card and waved me to proceed toward the gangway and out on American soil, where Uncle George, my father's older brother was waiting for me. We took the subway and arrived in Astoria, Long Island where he lived with my Aunt Katina and their son Nick, a handsome, young boy of about 17 years of age, with blond hair and blue eyes. The stay in New York lasted ten days and was a most exciting and memorable experience. Uncle George and cousin Nick took me into Manhattan on several occasions and introduced me to the famous sights along Fifth, Sixth and Seventh Avenues. The most impressive thing during those excursions into the heart of New York was the imposing enormity of the skyscrapers, whose immensity I could not have been able to describe had I not seen them with my own eyes.

On the evening of May 28, 1947 I left New York by train for Chicago, Illinois where Uncle John met me at the Union Train Station at 9 A.M. the next morning.

Education has for its object the formation of character.
Herbert Spencer, *Social Statics, 1851.*

—— CHAPTER 2 ——

The College Years

UNCLE JOHN AND I arrived at his home, in Evanston, Illinois, a suburb of Chicago immediately to the north of the big city. Aunt Bettie, his wife, was waiting for us and she broke into a big smile and welcomed me in Greek, *kalos orises*, welcome. Friends of Uncle John and Aunt Bettie, Dr. and Mrs. Leften Stavrianos were also visiting that morning. Dr. Stavrianos was Professor of History and Mrs. Stavrianos Professor of Psychology at Northwestern University. They too joined in the excitement that my arrival had generated. Everyone was curious to learn about the economic and political situation in Greece, where a civil war was raging. Opening the presents that relatives in Greece had sent to Uncle John and Aunt Bettie was followed by oh's and ah's to express the satisfaction they felt.

Saturday, May 29, 1947, was the beginning of the traditional Memorial Day weekend. The week following Memorial Day weekend Uncle John began to discuss with me his plans for my starting college. In September I was to start attending Wright Junior College in Chicago.

He quickly became aware of my poor preparation in English and he decided that I spend the summer of 1947 concentrating on improving my new language skills. He bought me a method book entitled "English Self-Taught" and instructed me to begin studying the method daily, starting at 8:00 A.M in the morning and after a break for lunch to continue until six in the afternoon when he would be returning from his office. He reasoned that with him and Aunt Bettie as unofficial tutors, speaking to me in English and dissuading me from speaking Greek, I should be able to be ready to meet the demands of the freshman college year. The system of the "English Self-Taught" was beginning to bring improvements in my conversational English and use of proper grammar. Not too long after I started using the alarm clock to wake me up at 6:30 A.M., Uncle John told me that the alarm clock was too loud and that he was being awakened before his preferred time of 7:30 A.M. I found a way to muffle the sound of the alarm clock by enveloping it in a terry cloth hand towel, a process that allowed me to hear it but not Uncle John.

In September 1947, I started classes at the Wilbur Wright Junior College in Chicago. The College was located on the south west area of the city and to get there I had to take the Western Avenue street car, which began its route at the intersection of the beginning of Western Avenue and Howard Street that divided Chicago from the suburb of Evanston. At Addison and Western I boarded the west-bound Addison bus that took me by Wilbur Wright Junior College.

After graduating from Wright Junior College with a GPA of 3.8, I was accepted at Northwestern University in Evanston, Illinois, where I received a tuition scholarship.

I concentrated on premedical science courses, physics and chemistry, comparative anatomy, embryology and anthropology and one in economics, the latter to satisfy Uncle John's wish, who thought I should pursue business courses rather than premedical studies.

In the fall of 1949, I also met my future wife, Eugenia (Jane) Kutsunis, a native of Geneseo, Illinois and on November 24, Thanksgiving Day, we were married in Geneseo. The priest officiated at the ceremony in a Methodist church since the town did not have a Greek church. The priest had come from the Greek church in the neighboring city of Moline, Illinois.

The year at Northwestern University was full of exciting and learning experiences. Our classes were taught by the Chairs of the various departments and the delivery of lectures and their content were awe inspiring. At the end of the third year of college and university studies Jane and I moved to Geneseo, Illinois and I decided to do my fourth year of studies at Augustana College, located in Rock Island, Illinois, some 25 miles west of Geneseo.

In June 1951, I received my bachelor's degree in chemistry from Augustana College. I requested my chemistry professor, Dr. Hill, to allow me to take a summer course in biochemistry and he was more than happy to let me join him in his lab, where he was working on a contract from the U.S. Army to develop a number of aldehydes with antioxidant properties that could be tested in rubber used to make truck tires. The hope was that the addition of these compounds would reduce the chance of the tire being cracked in the cold environment of Alaska. I found out some time later from Professor Hill that one of the compounds I synthesized worked in preventing the cracking of the tires in very cold weather.

Research is the act of going up alleys
to see if they are blind.
Plutarch, *46-120 AD*

Success is not the result of spontaneous
combustion. You must set yourself on fire.
Reggie Leach, *Canadian hockey player, born 1950.*

CHAPTER 3

Opening The Road To Research

A BRILLIANT OPPORTUNITY

IN SEPTEMBER 1951, THE year before entering medical school, I
matriculated at the Graduate School of the University of Illinois in
Champaign-Urbana with a major in microbiology and a minor in
biochemistry. That academic year, 1951-1952, stands as a seminal year in
my subsequent career. The campus at Champaign-Urbana was a beehive
of research activity in several fields, including biochemistry, genetics,
microbiology, physics and chemistry. Outstanding scientists taught the

various science courses. Dr. Sol Spiegelman, a brilliant investigator, taught microbial genetics. He was a man of short stature, with curly hair and brown eyes. He was always pleasant and eager to answer questions at any time. His formal lectures were followed by organized evening sessions, that started after dinner and lasted until 10:30 p.m. He constantly challenged us with problems, proposed hypotheses and expected new experimental designs from each of us. He extracted the last ounce of ideas from our brains.

Dr. Spiegelman trained brilliant graduate students and fellows, who worked endlessly and performed the most imaginative experiments. One of the projects dealt with the production of bacterial mutants that lacked the ability to produce a given essential amino acid. This was accomplished by irradiating bacteria with ultra-violet light, which killed more than 99% of the culture and left some able to grow in a complete medium, i.e. a medium supplemented with all the essential amino acids. Using the "replicate plating" technique, we would identify colonies that were deficient in one or another amino acid by demonstrating their inability to grow in a medium which lacked a specific amino acid. These mutants would then be grown separately and their metabolic properties studied further.

Another course that fascinated me was synthesis of viruses and specifically of bacteriophage that was taught by Dr. Salvador Luria, another brilliant microbial geneticist, who in 1969 received the Nobel Prize in Physiology or Medicine. He was of average height, with sparse black hair and brown eyes. He always divided his day between his desk, where he was writing manuscripts, and his laboratory. I remember one day in the spring of 1952, while I was preparing bacteriologic media in the general lab, I saw Dr. Luria taking samples out of an International Preparatory Ultracentrifuge. He took a small plastic tube out of the rotor and with an excited voice, reminiscent of a young child who just solved a block puzzle, yelled at me, "Nick, Nick, look, I got it." What he showed me was what seemed like a speck of dirt at the bottom of the tube. That speck was his first evidence that he was able to synthesize bacteriophage. He quickly asked me not to discuss his findings with anyone, an obvious allusion to the fierce competition in the field. Dr. Luria's lectures on virology were fascinating because they were full of experimental data recently generated in his laboratory.

Young graduate students in Dr. Spiegelman's lab, like Halvorson and Campbell, were churning out the new data. I still remember one graduate student, whose name I cannot recall, working endless hours in a small cubicle, isolated from noise, outside air and interruptions, trying to isolate individual mutant yeast cells by using a hanging drop of growth medium, a glass pipette drawn to the size of a capillary tube and a stage that was moving using a pneumatic apparatus. I was indeed surrounded by dedicated people, who constantly asked questions about metabolic properties of bacteria, genetic factors to explain the synthesis of bacteriophage, and mechanisms of bacterial resistance to antibiotics.

The courses in biochemistry and genetics again brought me face-to-face with giants in their fields. Dr. William Rose, chair of Biochemistry, who discovered threonine, the last of the eight essential amino acids that people need but must get from food, gave the most lucid lectures on a complicated subject. Dr. Rhoads, chair of Genetics, taught our class how to make chromosomal preparations from corn flowers. The preparations were easy to make and we soon learned that we could identify the corn chromosomes from 1 to 10, based on their length and position of the centromere.

When the notice from the University of Illinois College of Medicine arrived in early 1952, informing me that I was accepted in medical school, I was determined to find opportunities to carry out research while studying medicine. I had not thought yet what specialty I was going to pursue but I felt that, if I could get involved in some research project, I would make use of the laboratory skills I had acquired during the year in Champaign-Urbana.

Fig. 1. Our family in Greece, 1946. I stand behind my father, Athanasios
and my mother, Alexandra. My brother Chris is next to me.

Fig. 2. In Athens, while my documents were being prepared. April, 1947.

Fig. 3. At a picnic outside of Athens. Iam on the left, Frangiskos Samaritas and his sister Louisa, on the right. Vaggelis Micromastoras to my left. April, 1947.

Fig. 4. On the liner "Saturnia," standing between two brides, on their way to meet their future husbands in America. May 9th, 1947.

Fig. 5. On the liner "Saturnia," with several Greek passengers.
I am standing on the second step. May 10th, 1947.

Fig .6. My cousin Nick Kefalides, son of Uncle George who lived in Astoria, New York. I am standing to his left. May 22nd, 1947.

Fig. 7. In Evanston, Illinois, summer 1947.

Nicholas A. Kefalides

Fig. 8. On the steps of Wilbur Wright Junior College, Chicago, Illinois, 1948.

Fig. 9. In front of Wilbur Wright Junior College. Dr. Argoe, professor of history, a Greek-American, among a group of classmates who had recently arrived from Greece. I am standing at the extreme right. 1949.

Fig. 10. With fellow graduate students at the University of Illinois, Urbana-Champaign. I am second from the left. November, 1951.

Fig. 11. At my desk, a graduate student at the University
of Illinois, Urbana-Champaign. November, 1951.

Crito, we owe a cork to Aesculapius.
Please, pay it and don't forget.
Socrates, in *Plato's Phaedo*, 5th century BC.

The highest activity a human being can attain is learning
for understanding, because to understand is to be free.
Baruch Spinoza, *17th Century*

CHAPTER 4

The Medical School Years

THE FIRST YEAR OF medical school began in September 1952 with a class of more than 160 students. There were only five women in our class. The two courses that many students dreaded were Anatomy, because of the strange Latin and Greek names and Biochemistry. Having had Latin and classical Greek in high school I found anatomy easier than most students.

Four students were assigned to each cadaver. We all had a syllabus, which helped with the dissection process. The anatomy lab reeked with the strong odor of formaldehyde. At the end of each session the strong odor permeated our white coats and our skin. Cadavers came in all sizes and degrees of fat padding. Anatomy was the reason one of our classmates, one of the four assigned to our cadaver, was totally intimidated by the uncertainty of the structures that lay below the skin. He was standing across from me during dissection and as we were ready to make our first incision he asked me how deep he should go into the skin. Looking at our cadaver, an emaciated, thin lady, I suggested he should not go too deep. I made my first incision and I was in the process of dissecting the skin from the trapezious muscle when a shriek from our partner pierced my ear as he shouted, "Nick, I think I hit bone!" I tried to quiet him and assure him that this was not surprising since the cadaver had no fat to separate the skin from the underlying muscle. Although he was not squeamish about handling a dead body, his subsequent behavior revealed an obvious lack of confidence in his ability to handle the complicated concepts of the various courses. The anatomy episode was a harbinger of what happened at the end of the first year. He decided to quit medical school and join a pharmaceutical company working as a detail man, visiting doctors in their offices and hospitals.

In my mind, the most dynamic and memorable teacher in our first year was the professor of anatomy, Dr. Zimmermann. He lectured with enthusiasm and tried to make the course as lively as possible even though we relied heavily on cadavers. With the flair of an artist, he would draw the course of nerves and blood vessels on his white coat with colored chalk. One time, he asked one of our classmates, Jerry Lewis, to take his shirt and undershirt off to show the distribution of back muscles on the student's athletic chest.

Having had two courses of biochemistry the year I was in Champaign-Urbana, made it easy again to deal with the general metabolic pathways and reactions of medical biochemistry.

Living quarters were not easy to find on the medical school campus in Chicago, Illinois. A new apartment building, that would allow students to rent a unit, was under construction and was to be ready in the spring of 1953. The University gave preference to married students and faculty and especially those with children.

During the first academic quarter, I lived at a medical fraternity house, while Jane was living in Geneseo, Illinois, helping in her father's clothing store. Not only freshmen lived in the fraternities, but also students from the more advanced classes, who were always available and eager to help first year students with their academic problems. In early spring of 1953, Jane joined me in Chicago and we moved into a small apartment on Jackson Boulevard, not far from the medical center. It was a one-bedroom apartment with a small kitchen and a bed that was raised and pushed inside the wall. Within a month after we moved to the Jackson Boulevard apartment, the University informed us that we could move to the staff apartments, into a "zero-bedroom unit". Zero-bedroom meant one room with two sofa-beds, a table with four chairs, a galley kitchen and one bathroom. Our small apartment faced west and we enjoyed the afternoon and evening sun. Jane found a good job in downtown Chicago, as a secretary to one of the vice presidents of Chicago Title and Trust Company. The elevated train that took her downtown stopped only a block away from our apartment building and made it easy for her to get to the station. The staff apartment building had a large number of tenants from our class, which offered us opportunities for get-togethers to study, play cards and for dinner parties. Fortunately, Jane's monthly salary was adequate to cover our basic needs and left enough for entertainment and incidentals.

The first year of medical school ended with a sense of great relief. Jane and I took a two-week vacation in Geneseo, where she helped in her father's store and I helped with odd jobs around the house.

We returned to Chicago, where Jane went back to work and I began working as a technician in the laboratory of the chairman of Biochemistry, Dr. Richard Winzler. This job was paying minimum wage and allowed students to continue working during the school year if they were maintaining a B or better grade average. With the onset of the second year, I continued to work part-time in the afternoons. Dr. Winzler's laboratory was involved in the isolation and characterization of serum glycoproteins and their changes seen in acute and chronic health disorders. Halfway into the year Dr. Winzler approached me and asked whether I would like to try my hand at a project of my own. I was told that the National Institutes of Health funded medical student part time research projects; I was happy to accept the offer.

My project would be to develop a new method of isolating and characterizing orosomucoid, a serum acid glycoprotein. In 1954, German scientists marketed a small free-flow electrophoresis apparatus that used the Schlieren optical system to follow the purity of precipitated fractions. I had devised a precipitation and fractionation system, using magnesium sulfate to isolate orosomucoid from Cohn's plasma fraction VI. Since the major component of plasma fraction VI is serum albumin, I had to eliminate it by precipitating it out. After several such steps and with the aid of the electrophoretic apparatus, that allowed me to follow the purity of orosomucoid, I was able to prepare pure fractions of the desired protein. I was able to photograph the image of the curve on the screen of the electrophoretic apparatus, using a built-in camera that used ordinary black and white film.

Since I only had a few hours in the afternoons to work in the lab, progress was slow until summer time when classes were off and I could work full time. The protein I had isolated was so pure, that with the help of Dr. M. Goodman and Mr. S. Silberberg of the Department of Pathology, we produced high titer antibodies against it in chickens. We used the antibodies to measure serum levels of orosomucoid in normal individuals and in those with acute or chronic diseases. These studies led to my Master's thesis and a publication in 1955, my very first, on the antibody serum levels of orosomucoid in health and disease. The article was published in "Proceedings of the Society for Experimental Biology and Medicine" (*Proc. Soc. Exptl. Biol. and Med.* 90: 641, 1955.)

In1956, I was awarded an M.S. degree in biochemistry, the same day I was awarded my M.D. In 1954, the Medical School gave each student a B.S. degree in Medicine. In 1956, in recognition of my research accomplishments, I was given the Borden Research Award in Medicine. It was a competitive event and I was the one selected. Nine years after arriving in the United States I received four degrees and a research award. This would have been unheard of in Greece in those years.

The second year of medical school was very demanding in time and effort. New courses explored the functions of the various organ systems; physiology opened the secrets of cardiac, lung and kidney functions and pathology analyzed the causes of disease and death by looking at normal and diseased tissue. Microbiology was the most fun for me since I already had a year of advanced microbial metabolism and genetics two years earlier in Champaign-Urbana. Pharmacology was a new area for almost the whole class and the mode of action of most of the commonly known drugs was unfolded in front of us, in lab experiments that used dogs and rabbits. Fortunately, we did not have to prepare the dogs for each experiment, something that was left to the lab technicians. If I had to select the two most fascinating courses in the second year, both in terms of new information and answering questions of system functions I would have to choose physiology and pharmacology.

It was in the second year that for the first time we were introduced to patients. The course was physical diagnosis known among students as PDOG. We were allowed to wear a short white jacket with our nametag, an early recognition of our ultimate goal. Young faculty introduced us to patients suffering from a variety of diseases and went over their clinical and physical findings. The emphasis was on exposing us to patients with cardiac, liver or lung problems where the physical findings were obvious to the naked eye or easily discernible on examination.

All the excitement and fascination with the second year courses was suddenly overshadowed and waned as the day of the comprehensive exam was approaching, an exam that covered the material we were taught during the first two years of classes. My classmate, Al Karkazis, and I reviewed the two-year course material diligently. It was a hard exam and I was pleased to learn that we both passed it. I was relieved and I took that as an excuse to take a long and needed summer vacation before I returned to the lab to continue on my research project.

In 1954, a very important event took place in my life. I became eligible to apply for U.S. citizenship. In the application there was a space to indicate a change of name. In all the time that I had lived in the USA, people kept mispronouncing my last name or simply did not bother to pronounce it and called me by my first name. I decided to change my last name from Kefalides to Alexander, to honor my mother's first name "Alexandra." About two months before I was to appear before a judge, in Henry County, Illinois, Jane and I attended a garden party at Dr. Winzler's home in Hinsdale Illinois, a suburb of Chicago. A young, ten year old child, and her parents who were attending the same party were introduced to me. A month later we met the same family at another party and without hesitation, the child said "Hello Mr. Kefalides", remembering my name and pronouncing it correctly. On the day I was to take the oath, the judge asked me if I wanted to make any last minute changes. I asked that, Alexander, stay as my middle name and Kefalides remain as my last name. In the process, I gained a new middle name and kept my family name.

The third and fourth years of medical school took us out of the labs and into the clinics. We rotated through the different services of the Research and Educational Hospitals and we were assigned to residents of the particular service such as internal medicine, surgery, urology, pediatrics, hematology, ophthalmology, otorhino-laryngology and neurology.

The whole atmosphere on the wards and clinics was more relaxed and we were eager to see patients who presented with the signs and symptoms we were reading about in our textbooks. These were the years when we got to know our professors better. I began to know better the professors in medicine and surgery, as well as the residents in both services. The formal lectures were few and involved specialized topics with small numbers of students attending. In our senior year we occasionally took night call with one of the interns in our service, a practice that was preparatory for our internships the following year.

Graduation day arrived in June 1956. The Schools of Medicine, Dentistry and Pharmacy as well as the Graduate School graduates gathered in the assembly hall and as each student's name was called we approached the stage where we were given our medical diplomas. I had the unique opportunity to march a second time to receive my Master of Science degree in Biochemistry. My wife Jane and Uncle John were present at the ceremony. Hugs and kisses were in order as we met outside the hall. Uncle John took photographs to commemorate the successful outcome of four years of intensive study. Several of our classmates got together in small groups to congratulate and wish each other good luck in their internships. The majority of graduates selected hospitals away from the city and in different states. I was accepted into the internship program of the University of Illinois Research and Educational Hospitals in Chicago. The internship year was fantastic, with excellent opportunities to develop independent actions under the tutelage of brilliant faculty.

I had decided to pursue a residency program in internal medicine. I had applied for it at the same hospital and I was accepted. However, my residency had to wait three years. Having been deferred from military service because of my studies, I now had to decide which service to apply for. In early 1957 I applied for the air force. Soon after I applied, my medical school advisor and friend, Dr. Mark Lepper, asked me to consider applying for the US Public Health Service at NIH. The Chief of the Department of Medicine, Dr. Harry Dowling called me to his office and he also urged me to consider applying to NIH. At that time I had little knowledge of the many functions of NIH. I knew that it was composed of several institutes carrying out research in several disease areas, such as arthritis, skin diseases, diabetes, cancer, blood diseases, dentistry and cardiovascular disorders. Over the years, as a grade school and high school student and later as a college and medical student I had developed an attitude of respect, admiration and a sense of obedience for some of my teachers. It was hard for me to say no to their suggestions and sent in my application to NIH. In early spring the air force informed me of my acceptance in their program and NIH did the same the following day. By this time, Drs. Dowling and Lepper described in general terms the nature of the project that I was supposed to be involved with.

NIH had initiated a project to study the effects of salt solution in the prevention and treatment of shock during the first 72 hours following a skin burn. When I indicated that I had not worked with patients in shock, Dr. Dowling revealed more of the NIH project. The shock was no longer a problem but rather fatal septicemia, due to antibiotic resistant *staphylococcus aureus* and *pseudomonas aeruginosa*. The big news was that the project was being carried out in Lima, the capital of Peru. It sounded intriguing and challenging to say the least. I had never traveled outside the USA and Jane was very much against living in a South American country that she considered underdeveloped and very foreign. As much as I was becoming interested in the idea of joining NIH, Jane was set against it. The impasse brought in Dr. Lepper, who walked all the way to our apartment to persuade Jane to go with me to Peru. I wasn't present when Dr. Lepper, talked to Jane but she related to me the arguments he used to convince her. He said it would be an excellent opportunity to run a research project and a great chance to further my career. Jane relented and I accepted the NIH offer. On July 1, 1957, we moved to Bethesda, Maryland.

We are in the midst of a cold war,
which is getting warmer.
Bernard Baruch, *Speech Before the US*
Senate Committee, 1948.

———— CHAPTER 5 ————

Concerns And Fears Of The Cold War

THE GENESIS OF THE PERU BURN PROJECT

IN 1945, AFTER THE atomic bombs were dropped on Hiroshima and Nagasaki, the world entered the nuclear era. By the late 1940's and early 1950's the Soviet Union and China were also developing capabilities to manufacture and deliver nuclear weapons. The United States government thus faced the possibility of having to take care of large numbers of civilian casualties in the event of a nuclear attack or nuclear accident. In the defense department's war scenarios, the prospects for "surviving" a nuclear exchange depended in part on the medical resources that would remain available following such an attack. It was estimated that with the limited number of physicians, and with the potential for some 32 million casualties following a nuclear attack, there would be roughly one physician for every 600 patients. Data from recent conventional wars was used to estimate the trauma-related blood requirements in a post-nuclear war society. These calculations resulted in a projected disparity between need and availability of medical resources that was astounding and daunting to defense and public health officials. It was challenging to develop an effective medical response for the surviving injured.

In 1950, the United States had no centralized facilities in which to care for large numbers of trauma or burn cases, save for one facility at the Brook Army Medical Center, in San Antonio, Texas. That same year, the Surgery Study Section of the National Institutes of Health published a recommendation in which it was strongly suggested that "The oral use of saline solution is adopted as standard procedure in the treatment of shock due to burns and other serious injuries in the event of large-scale civilian catastrophe," (Public Health Reports, 1950; 65:1317-1320]. It was "the consensus of the 1950 Surgery Study Section that on the basis of the animal work done by Dr. S.M. Rosenthal of the National Institutes of Health and the clinical work done bay Drs. Carl A. Moyer and Charles Fox and others, the efficacy of such treatment was demonstrated...."

As a result of treating battle casualties during World War II, the use of plasma was shown to be efficient in the prevention and treatment of shock. The answer to the question "Why try another mode of therapy if blood and plasma worked?" was simple; there was not enough blood and plasma to meet the needs of massive casualties in the event of nuclear attack or accident.

To carry out the clinical studies the government decided to go outside the United States, to Central and South America, where hospital facilities were few in the big cities and all burn cases were cared for in one or two hospitals rather than in every neighborhood hospital as in the United States. The National Research Council sent out a committee of surgeons and scientists to visit the capitals of some of these countries and make arrangements to set up the clinical study sites where oral and intravenous saline solution would be tested and compared with intravenous plasma and other modes of therapy in the treatment of burn patients. The committee chose Lima, Peru as a study site where all the burn patients were taken to one of three main hospitals, the Men's, the Women's or the Children's. The only other burn facility in the city was the armed forces hospital that did not cater to private individuals. The arrangement was made with the Dean of the Medical School of the University of San Marcos, Dr. Alberto Hurtado. Hurtado was Peruvian but educated and trained in the United States. He was a 1924 graduate of Harvard Medical School and an intern at Boston City Hospital from 1925 to 1926.

The project started in Lima in the summer of 1951. Its headquarters was set up at the Women's Hospital. The Director of the project was an American Public Health Service Commissioned Officer, Dr. Kehl Markley, a young surgeon. Except for Dr. Markley, all of the project staff was Peruvian, including the hospital surgeons, the nurses, the physicians who ran the biochemistry and microbiology labs and the pathologist who performed the autopsies. It should be pointed out that in the 1950's the idea of random selection of patients to one or another treatment arm was not applied nor was the practice of obtaining a patient's informed consent entertained. Informed patient consent prior to entry into clinical research trials did not become a standard of research protocols in the United States until 1974.

In the Lima burn project, patients were placed on a particular treatment arm on an alternate case basis. When an adult or child was brought in the hospital, the family left their patient to the mercy of the doctors. The families I met had complete trust in the doctor and asked no questions. The burn project was there to save lives and the American government was paying all the expenses. The financial arrangement was simple. The NIH grant went to the University of San Marcos, where Dr. Hurtado kept an amount of dollars corresponding to the indirect cost (overhead) and the direct cost was deposited in the American Bank in Lima in the name of the American project director. In the current case the funds were deposited in my name. This money was used to pay salaries for the surgeons, the nurses and nurses' aids, the chiefs of labs as well as for supplies for the clinical labs. The level of monthly salary was significantly higher for all project employees than that paid by the Peruvian Department of Public Health. Fortunately, there was no overt evidence of resentment by those not working for the project. Needless to say, all physicians were allowed to carry on with their private practices but whenever new burn patients arrived, they were obligated to take care of those cases until their blood pressure was stabilized and the appropriate biochemical and bacteriologic tests were performed.

Studies published by Kehl Markley and the Peruvian colleagues demonstrated the efficacy of saline solution therapy in burn shock. The effect of saline administration was as good as the more expensive plasma in preventing death from shock during the first 72 hours. While the use of saline with and without plasma was proving to be very effective in preventing death from shock, the project team began to notice a gradual increase of bacteremias and septicemias as the years progressed. The principal bacterial strains, which led to fatal septicemias, were *staphylococcus aureus and pseudomonas aeruginosa.*

Dr. Rosenthal and his colleagues at NIH began to look for ways to stem this trend of fatal septicemias and began experiments using a mouse model where the mice were scalded in hot water, then treated with combinations of antibiotics and pooled human gamma globulin. The results demonstrated a significant degree of protection against infection and death from staphylococcus and pseudomonas.

In 1956, an important scientific event occurred, the availability of the polio vaccine. Up until then, before the vaccine became available, pooled human gamma globulin was the only pharmacologic agent given to patients with polio to help stem progression of the disease. The American Red Cross was in control of all available quantities of globulin and dispensed it accordingly. With the development of the polio vaccine the Red Cross was left with enormous quantities of pooled human gamma globulin and was looking for ways to "get rid of it." Dr. Rosenthal made a simple request and the Red Cross was more than willing to supply NIH with all the gamma globulin it needed. The scientific group in charge of the burn project at NIH modified the treatment regimen, which now included saline solution, saline solution plus plasma, saline solution plus gamma globulin and saline solution combined with plasma plus gamma globulin. The gamma globulin solution was to be given in 1 ml per kilogram of body eight, intramuscularly on admission and repeated on the third and fifth day. All patients were to receive antibiotics on a prophylactic basis.

Within a week after our arrival in Lima a large number of vials of pooled human globulin arrived from NIH and within a day the new regimen was put into effect.

My role in the project, as director, was to carry on, not only the day to day administrative duties but also supervise the use of salt solution and plasma and the addition of human gamma globulin in the existing regimens, as well.

Let Observation with Extensive View,
Survey Mankind from China to Peru.
Samuel Johnson, *The Vanity of Human Wishes, 1749.*

CHAPTER 6

Beginning Life In Peru

IN JULY, 1957, PRESIDENT Eisenhower commissioned me in the U.S. Public Health Service with the rank of Lieutenant or Surgeon; my rank was elevated to Lieutenant Commander the same month I was sent to Peru. My wife, Jane, and I were issued special passports, conferring a status between regular and diplomatic ones. We spent our first month visiting NIH in Bethesda, Maryland and I received instructions on the procedures of the Peruvian research project initiated by Dr. Rosenthal and the other senior scientists at NIH. Dr. Markley, who was working at Dr. Rosenthal's laboratory at the time, was very helpful and provided me with information about the project, the Peruvian doctors and the technical staff working on the project as well as about life in Peru. He briefed me on the Director of the Children's Hospital, Dr. Gilberto Morey, who recognized the importance of the project and was very much in favor of providing us with lab supplies and administrative support.

At the end of July 1957, Jane and I began our trip to Lima, Peru. We first stopped in New York, where we spent a few days opening a checking account with the Bank of New York that had a branch in Lima and where the grant funds were deposited. The U.S. government agreed to ship our 1956 model Chevrolet sedan to Lima at their expense and we arranged for delivery of the car to one of the docks in New York. We flew first class out of Idelwild Airport (now John F. Kennedy Airport) on a Panagra DC-7 airliner.. The trip was long and tiresome. We stopped in Miami and then in Panama City where we were allowed to deplane. As the plane door opened and we began to go down the mobile steps and into the night I felt an oppressive, hot and humid sensation enveloping my body. I felt my clothes clinging onto my skin. It was my first exposure to a tropical climate. Within a minute I heard Jane murmur to me, "Is this where you are going to bring me?" I assured her that Lima was further south and not at all tropical. Early the next morning we stopped at Quito, Ecuador. We stepped out of the plane again and what struck me and Jane was the emptiness of the airfield. There were wads of dry weeds tumbling along the tarmac. Again, Jane expressed her dismay.

When we finally arrived in Lima, we could see a large airport facility. The plastic surgeon at the Children's Hospital, Dr. Augusto Bazan and Dr. Manuel Bocanegra, the internist, were there to meet us and take us to our hotel in the center of the city. The hotel had been only recently renovated and the rooms were freshly painted. The walls of our room were olive green and because of the high humidity we could see droplets of water on the wall. This was wintertime south of the equator and the chill in the air was penetrating.

Later in the afternoon of the day of arrival, Dr. Bocanegra picked us up and drove us to the Children's Hospital to meet some of the clinical staff, nurses and orderlies, and the physicians in charge of the clinical and microbiology labs. Everyone seemed happy to see us and meet us and wished us a pleasant stay. That same afternoon, Dr. Bazan took us to the Surgical Pavilion, where 12 beds were exclusively used in one of the rooms for the care of burn patients in the study. All the beds were occupied. Only patients with 10% or more of their body surface area burned were admitted to the study.

On just the second day after our arrival we found a nice one bedroom apartment in San Isidro, one of the most desirable suburbs in Lima. Our household effects had been shipped by air and they had arrived before we did and were put into storage at the Children's Hospital. In only a few days, Jane and I were settled in our new home.

San Isidro is studded with beautiful villas, with tropical and subtropical trees, gardens full of flowering bushes and well-manicured lawns. Our apartment was part of a complex of six apartments arranged around a small courtyard. Jane and I went out to buy bedroom furniture at a large shopping center called "Todos," that had been built by the Rockefeller Foundation. The center featured a Sears and Roebuck department store, a large supermarket and a variety of small shops.

We furnished our living room with a set of two easy chairs and a sofa from a special boutique called "Oeschle." The upholstery fabric was a unique design by Sylvia Von Hagen, wife of author Victor Von Hagen, who used the locally produced linen and produced a beautiful pattern she called "Cathedral Windows." The colors were striking – blue, black and green on a white background. Some of our other furniture was more improvised and drawn from local markets. We created bookcases by separating wooden boards on piles of red bricks. We found beautiful oil paintings of bullfights that we used to decorate the walls of the living room. We managed to furnish our apartment in a satisfactory and attractive way. With time we bought carvings of Inca Indian heads of mahogany and other types of sculpture depicting native designs. A small super market and a private grocery store, the bodega, were within a block of our apartment building. Until our car arrived from the States, we used public transportation or the ever-present "collectivos," the old, dilapidated cars that functioned as shared taxis and could be used by five different passengers.

DAILY ACTIVITIES IN LIMA

The research protocol of our study required that when a patient arrived I had to be notified, day or night, so that I could supervise the patient's assignment to the proper treatment arm. In addition to myself, the surgeon of the hospital where the patient was taken, whether at the Women's, the Men's or Children's, was also notified so that the burn areas were cleaned and dressed. Dr. Augusto Bazan was the surgeon in charge at the Children's Hospital, where all burned children were admitted. Dr. Manuel Bocanegra, the project physician for all three hospitals and Dr. Pedro Stastny, also a physician, in charge of biochemical studies for all three hospitals, were also notified. Dr. Jose Arana, the microbiologist in the project, was also present to take the initial wound cultures, as well as blood, urine and stool cultures.

Every admission represented a slice of the social structure of life in Lima. Here was a mother or a father bringing a young child, severely burned, crying in pain. The parent looked at the nurses and doctors with pleading eyes, surrendering the life of their child to the people, who to them were supposed to be "miracle workers." The majority of the children came from shantytown areas that surrounded the northern and eastern parts of Lima. Their homes were no more than one-room huts with corrugated tin roofs. These huts served as sleeping quarters, kitchens, and places to heat water for washing and bathing. In these closed quarters it was easy for a young child to accidentally fall on an open fire, resulting in a serious burn. Another common source of burns among adults was the fire generated by maids working in a house and trying to melt the wax in order to polish the wooden floors using a kerosene torch, at times resulting in a sudden fire and severe burns.

Parents brought their severely burned children to the hospital and left them to the mercy of the doctors, without knowing what was to happen to them, without having any idea of the kind of treatment they were about to receive, unaware of the clinical research project that they were participating in—seeking to determine whether the protective gamma globulin or the saline solution alone might stave off shock, infection, or septicemia. The parents were not asked whether they permitted the doctors and the hospital to submit their child to an experimental procedure. In other words, there was no opportunity for an informed consent, a required procedure today. This is not surprising for that time, since the concept and application of protection of the individual from the risks of research was not yet practiced in the United States or anywhere else. The only thing the parents were assured of was that their child was going to receive the best treatment available, irrespective of the fact that they had no idea what the best or worse therapy was. The same applied for the adults. Even if they were not in shock and were able to communicate, they were not given an explanation of what kind of treatment they were going to receive, whether saline solution alone, saline solution plus plasma or saline and gamma globulin. What impressed me most was the absolute faith the parents of the burned children as well as the burned adults had towards the hospital personnel. The other impressive thing was that in the course of the six years since the project was initiated, the professional personnel had developed a perfect routine of study in handling each patient. If a patient died, it was the result of two main factors: the extent of the surface area burned and whether there was staphylococcus or pseudomonas septicemia. All burned patients, especially young children had another thing against them, they behaved as individuals with reduced immune defenses, irrespective of the age and the level of gamma globulin in their serum.

Soon after we arrived in Lima, I began to study Spanish by taking private lessons from a local teacher whose English was excellent. I picked up Spanish quickly and within two months I was able to master the grammar and be able to form sentences with great facility. I, therefore, stopped my formal lessons. A major factor with my success to learn the language quickly was my knowledge of Greek, whose pronunciation of words is, as in Spanish, phonetic and after hearing a word I could immediately form a mental picture of it. My daily contact with the hospital personnel forced me to converse in Spanish and my ability to speak it well resulted in an invitation to give my first lecture to the house staff on the rational use of antibiotics, in Spanish, six months after my arrival. My love for the Spanish language persists even today, and more than 54 years later, when I have an opportunity, I make use of it.

Jane befriended several American women, whose husbands were working with a variety of mining and oil companies or with the US economic development program, "Point Four." This gave her an opportunity to be involved in a variety of activities, including theater, bridge, bowling, painting classes, archeological digging and silver and copper metal work. Mementos of Jane's social and cultural activities that survive today include a sterling silver dish with the inscription from the bowling club, "Most Improved Bowler", several "wacos" (pots uncovered in old Chancay Indian graves), and a child's blanket, wrapped around a mummy which she had framed. She has a memorable collection of silver dishes, ashtrays, iced tea spoons, a large copper plate with a silver Incan symbol for November (the month of our wedding) in the center and a copper wall mask of an Incan Puma cat – all hand filed and hammered by her over the three years we were in Lima.

We made longstanding friendships with several of the American families living in Lima. Lee Stalker (the President of Sears Roebuck in Peru) and his wife Helen, Dr. and Mrs. Howard Mortensen (of the University of Wisconsin), Dr. Fred and Marion Daggett (of the University of New Hampshire), Arthur and Lucille Herskovits (representing Warner Brothers Pictures in Lima), Irwin and Cynthia Marks (representing Columbia Pictures in Lima), Henry Bonifacio and Bridgit (representing 20th Century Fox in Lima) and Gloria and Norman Holmes (working for an American copper company.) A most memorable couple was Elsa and Karl Heumann, a retired couple who fled Germany before the war and who were one of the most hospitable couples in Lima.

For Jane and me, the years in Lima were memorable for all the social gatherings and fine food. There were frequent dinner parties, weekend drives into the countryside and weekly bridge parties. Practically every weekend we gathered with friends to enjoy a home cooked meal—usually a fusion of Peruvian and American cuisine. We enjoyed trying South American dishes and in a short time, the country's staples became our standard fare. Arroz con Pollo (rice with chicken) made with quality ingredients was a favorite as well as sea bass which was prepared in a richly flavored tomato sauce. We were introduced to a classical Spanish dish "Paella" which has its origin in Valencia, Spain. There are three varieties of paella: Valencian paella, which consists of white rice, green vegetables, meat (usually chicken or duck), beans and seasonings. Seafood paella replaces meat with seafood and omits beans and green vegetables. Mixed paella is a combination of meat, seafood and vegetables. The seafood dish we immediately fell in love with was the appetizer Ceviche made with marinated Corvina and topped with diced onion, lemon juice and chili peppers.

With our friends and fellow Americans, the Morrison's and Mortensen's we explored the interior of the country. There were many memorable trips. We took the long, winding railroad to Huancayo, 17,000 feet up in the Andes. The train made a zig-zag track along the side of the mountain until it reached its destination. Huancayo is a small town that typified life in the mountain towns. Almost everyone, man, woman and child, was wearing colorful hats and outfits while moving herds of llamas through the streets.

On the day of our arrival to Huancayo, we made the mistake of taking a stroll for a couple of blocks. We soon found out that we could not carry out a simple conversation, and became short of breath from the low oxygen in the air. Some in our party developed severe neck pain and headaches and there were episodes of explosive diarrhea. The locals told us it was the "cirroche", high altitude sickness. We had not rested the recommended 40-60 minutes to adjust to the high altitude.

Our trip to Cuzco and Machu Picchu, which means Ancient Peak, a year later, with Cynthia Marks, was totally different. We flew with a local airline, called Fawcett, to Cuzco. As we approached the high altitudes of the Andes we were asked to use rubber tubes that extended from the seatbacks and breathe in oxygen. The system, although primitive, worked well. When we landed in Cuzco we were advised to rest in bed for about one hour before attempting to walk around. This time, we did follow the advice and noted no effects of mountain sickness. We spent the first day visiting the old city and the ruins of Sacsayhuaman, a fortress constructed of massive stones that were held together without mortar, an engineering and architectural feat. The question I recall from that visit that still puzzles historians is, how did the Incas bring all those massive stones from a distant mountain when it is known that they were not using the wheel, even though they knew of its existence? There are different theories but no firm answers.

The trip to Machu Picchu, the next day, was a treasured experience. For part of the journey we used a local train and then a bus that was considerably more modern than the bridge over a small river that we had to cross. As buses increased in width, the appropriate changes in the width of the bridge were neglected and invariably the sides of the buses could be heard scraping the walls of the bridge. The bus brought us to a clearing that stood in front of the ruins of the majestic city Machu Picchu that was rediscovered in 1911 by Hiram Bingham. Machu Picchu was unknown to the Spaniards. The view beyond the old city is breathtaking, with green foliage-covered mountain peaks looming towards the sky.

INTERESTING EPIDEMIOLOGIC DATA

The burn project was coming along well with the expected results. The effect of pooled human globulin had little effect in protecting adults and older children against staphylococcus or pseudomonas septicemia. But, in preschool children, with burns covering up to 30% of body surface area, the use of saline solution plus gamma globulin was effective in protecting against septicemias in up to 35 of patients. This regimen was not significantly better than saline solution plus plasma; however, the combination of saline solution plus plasma and gamma globulin seemed to have a superior effect. Among young children who developed pseudomonas septicemia, death was the ultimate outcome, except in one case. It was a young girl, about 10 or 11 years old named Ana del Aguila, who had severe burns and developed pseudomonas septicemia. To everyone's surprise, she pulled through, underwent skin grafts and eventually went home. Another patient was a little boy, maybe six or seven years old, named Cesar, who survived a staphylococcus septicemia and underwent skin grafts and eventually went home. In all these cases of patients that survived infections, it was the skill and dedication of the plastic surgeon, Dr. Augusto Bazan that was mainly responsible for their ultimate survival and discharge home. The colonization by pseudomonas of the burn skin of children hospitalized in the burn unit was an absolute certainty. Adjacent to the burn unit was the "sala general" "the general ward," where all kinds of surgical cases were being treated. We carried out skin cultures of the surgical scars from several of these non-burn patients and we found many of them to be colonized either by *staphylococcus aureus or pseudomas aeruginosa* or both and yet not one of them ever developed septicemia. Obviously, the burn itself contributed to the increased susceptibility of the burn patients, probably by reducing their immune defenses.

One day I received a call from the American Ambassador in Peru, Mr. Theodore Achilles, who asked me to allow the transfer of two sisters, 14 and 15 years of age, They were both burn victims, being cared for in a hospital in a remote mountain town. The local surgeon managed to keep the sisters alive and their involved skin areas dry and free of bacterial growth. But there was no one in the immediate vicinity with the skills to do the skin transplants. Somehow the reputation of the burn project reached the remote village and through some means the village surgeon asked the Ambassador to intercede and faciliate the transfer to Lima. Although I had explained to Mr. Achilles that moving these two girls to the Children's Hospital in Lima was not a very prudent decision because of the high probability of bacterial septicemia, he pushed me to accept the two patients and I acquiesced. When the sisters arrived in Lima we saw two young teenagers, alert, without fever and with dry burn areas covered with a pink scab, the pink color arising from the liquid sulfa medication their surgeon sprayed over their wounds. We did the appropriate cultures and we were struck by the lack of staphylococcus or pseudomonas. We placed them in the treatment groups that were called for. Their wounds were treated properly and to no one's surprise within a week their wound were colonized by pseudomonas, and by the second week they developed pseudomonas septicemia. The antibiotics we had then, polymycin-B and Colistin were ineffectual and sadly, they both died. In retrospect, we could have chosen alternative approaches that might have saved the two sisters. Dr. Bazan could have traveled to the mountain town and carried out the skin transplants there, then followed them for a week or two and then returned them to the care of their local surgeon. Another alternative would have been to have kept the two sisters out of the research project and admit them to a regular ward, thus avoiding contact with the dreadful pseudomonas strain and allowing eventual skin grafting. The American Ambassador was deeply saddened when he learned of the bad outcome.

*As the traveler who has once been from home
is wiser than he who has never left his own
doorstep, so a knowledge of one other culture
should sharpen our ability to scrutinize more
steadily, to appreciate more lovingly our own.*
Margaret Mead, *Coming of Age in Samoa*, 1928.

CHAPTER 7

Our Social And Cultural Activities

JANE ARRIVED IN LIMA in a very anxious and negative frame of mind. Fortunately, there was much to keep her busy – selecting an apartment, buying furniture, learning how to shop for groceries in a strange country, and learning her way around the city. It was harder for her since she didn't speak a word of Spanish when we arrived. But she picked up the language quickly and once she learned some basic Spanish, she became more confident.

Lima, with its rich ancient history and its vibrant cultural scene offered many opportunities to develop new interests and hobbies. The Union Church in Lima had a large group of Americans in diverse fields of business and social activities. It was there that one had the opportunity to meet Americans and to join a bridge club, sign up for art classes, learn to bowl and audition for the Lima Theatre Workshop.

We were surprised to learn that we could have access to ancient Incan burial grounds and we could explore them like archaeologists. In the desert on the western coast of Peru, which extended for a few miles, one could arrange with the official guards to probe the ground with narrow metal rods looking for places to dig. Since there were no postings of the tombs, the routine was to drop the metal probe in a random fashion into several spots hoping that the rod would touch a clay pot thus producing a characteristic ping sound, which prompted the "amateur archeologist" with the aid of the guard to dig with a shovel, until the object was revealed. The most common findings were ceremonial pots, containing corn and a clay drinking cup in which chicha, an alcoholic beverage, was added, presumably for the dead have to have some nourishment in the afterlife.

Some of the most rewarding experiences came about when Jane joined groups of Americans on archaeological expeditions, or exploring the many elegant department stores and jewelry stores. The owners of the most elegant jewelry shop introduced her to the local "maestro," a silver smith who designed and made the most elegant silver jewelry and flatware. She was able to design and learned to form several silver and copper pieces in his studio that we treasure today.

Sylvia Von Hagen, designed and hand printed on the local Peruvian linen her extraordinary Peruvian designs that were used to upholster modern furniture. We still have some of the furniture we purchased in Lima.

We have many memories from Lima. We faced challenges while adjusting to life in Peru, but we also recall their endearing customs. Some of the most notable were: if a street or road developed a "pot hole", you would see a large red geranium plant covering the hole – no sign, just the red plant! Jane had to wash clothes in the kitchen sink. If the weather was clear and sunny she could hang the washing on the top floor of the building where the "Portero", the building guardian lived. She then had to monitor the stairs to make sure thieves did not steal the laundry.

One annoying problem was the flea situation in Lima. Curiously, if we went to a movie with friends, typically everyone else would leave the theater without noticing any flea bites. But Jane not only would find herself bitten, but would also find fleas would be in the seams of her clothing. Upon arriving home she would have to strip out of her clothes in the hallway before entering the living room and spray and shake out her clothing.

One experience that traumatized Jane to the degree that she has never felt comfortable in deep water occurred while we were with Peruvian friends enjoying a picnic and swimming excursion on the beach along the Pacific coast. Jane ventured out into the water and suddenly she was caught in an undertow. We all stood by ready to help her but she regained her footing and returned to shore. She has never gone swimming since that experience – and will walk along the beach or wade in shallow water – but nothing more.

But by far the most enduring memories from Lima are the parties—particularly my birthday party. Our Peruvian colleagues, like most Peruvians, enjoyed celebrating holidays, especially birthdays. The custom relies on secrecy, for it is the wife of the celebrant who is in on the "surprise" visit by the husband's friends and colleagues at midnight of the eve of his birthday. In my case, Jane had discreetly spent the day preparing all kinds of food and hors d' oeuvres and buying abundant quantities of pisco (the Peruvian equivalent of gin or ouzo) and soft drinks. At about one or two minutes before the stroke of midnight the band, standing in front of the house, began to play " Happy Birthday to You" with all the visiting guests singing along.

Another similar event occurred with the birthday of Dr. Gabriel Gurmendi, who worked for the project at the Women's Hospital. When the well wishers arrived outside Dr, Gourmendi's house and the small band began to play "Happy Birthday,"

Mrs. Gurmendi opened the window and with a surprising look at her face she shouted *"Hola, que sorpresa. Gracias por su visita. El doctor va abrir la puerta"*. (Hi, what a surprise. Thank you for your visit. The doctor will open the door.)

Once inside Dr. Gurmendi's house, all the visitors embraced him and his wife and wished them a "Happy Birthday." Immediately after that, everyone descended on the food and the drinks. The atmosphere was festive, and noisy. In this particular event I was still not used to drinking pure pisco. I had tried pisco sour, a mild cocktail and I liked it. As the night progressed, I noticed some of the Peruvian colleagues pouring their drink into one of the several large flowerpots while they insisted that I continue to drink. The next surprise of the night came when Jane and I decided to leave. We quickly found out that the doors were locked and no one was permitted to leave until the end of the party. Finally, our colleague, Dr. Manuel Bocanegra, devised an escape. He threw Jane's purse surreptitiously out the window and in a surprise move Jane, Dr. Bocanegra and I bolted out of the house and into his car. As we were speeding toward our house, a car was pursuing us, it's driver honking its horn and flashing its lights. After a while the chase car gave up and we returned to our home sated but not drunk.

Cold is the heart, fair Greece! That looks on thee,
Nor feels as lovers o'er the dust they loved; Dull is
the eye that will not weep to see Thy walls defaced,
thy moldering shrines removed By British hands.
Lord Byron: *Childe Harold's Pilgrimage*

CHAPTER 8

Our Trip To Europe

IN THE SPRING OF 1959, Jane and I planned a 45-day summer vacation to Europe, to include visits to England, France, Germany, Switzerland, Greece and Italy. Both of us were yearning for this sojourn for a variety of reasons. It would be an unparalleled opportunity to visit Europe for the first time in our lives, for me to visit Greece for the first time in 12 years and for Jane to meet my family. Jane had already visited Greece in 1947, alone.

From Lima we traveled to Washington, D.C., where I spent a few days in the laboratory of Dr. Rosenthal reviewing the status of the Lima burn project. It was during that visit that he offered me the opportunity to stay a third year in Peru as director of the project. Even though this meant postponing the start of my residency back in Illinois, I accepted the offer. The most compelling reason for me, to work an additional third year in Lima, was the need to collect additional data so that we could have a better statistical basis for comparing the various treatment groups in the study. With a greater number of patients enrolled in the study-a larger "n" value in the parlance of statisticians- we could clarify the benefit of human Gamma Globulin and its effect on susceptibility to bacterial septicemia.

From Washington, D.C., we traveled to New York City where we spent a few days touring the sites in downtown Manhattan. After the short stay we traveled to Idlewild International Airport to board a TWA DC-7 bound for Europe. (Idlewild International Airport was renamed John F. Kennedy International Airport one month after the assassination of the president in November 1963.)

Our first stop was London. There were countless sights to visit and we started with the most obvious ones; we visited Big Ben, the House of Parliament, Piccadilly Circus, and Trafalgar Square. The most unique sight beside the statue of Lord Nelson in the square was the swarm of pigeons that were either perched on the lions at the base of the column or would waddle around the visitors waiting for someone to throw seeds or peanuts or anything that a bird might consider edible. And we did some window shopping; we could not escape Harrod's, the ultimate store with an innumerable variety of specialty shops and a range of costly and not-so-costly items, the food market and the famous buffet restaurant.

We had obtained the address of one of my former classmates, Alekos Andreadis, who was specializing in neurosurgery in London. Seeing him again after all these years, was quite emotional. We embraced and gave each other a big hug. Jane and I were introduced to his wife, a beautiful woman he married in Greece. We spent hours reminiscing about our school years together and our subsequent careers. The next day, Alekos and his wife invited us to go see a play in London "Irma La Deuce". This magnificent, romantic comedy was eventually made into a movie in 1963, with Shirley MacLaine, as Irma La Deuce; the movie was a huge success and to this day, always reminds me of my reunion with my former childhood classmate.

Our next stop was Paris. The architectural and physical beauty of the city was captivating. and we immediately fell in love with it. We found Parisians to be as beautiful as the city was enchanting. We enjoyed touring the old arondissements, squares and gardens and relaxing in sidewalk cafes.

My only high school classmate living in Paris was Jo Saporta, a Holocaust survivor. We called him, announced our arrival and he was surprised and excited to hear my voice after fifteen years. We got together the next day and we toured a few must-see sites, such as the Louvre, in addition to the "grand magasines," Galleries Lafayette and Printemps and the specialty boutiques. That evening Jo and his brother took us to see the Follies Bergeres. The beautiful dancing girls and the excitement of the audience made the night a memorable experience.

Our next destination after Paris was Dusseldorf. I am not sure why Dusseldorf was added to the itinerary but it's obvious that an unknowing travel agent in Lima had arranged it. When compared to London and Paris Dusseldorf appeared dreary as we traveled by cab to the hotel.

The regimentation that was pounded into the minds of the German people during the years of the Nazi control became immediately evident as we tried to take a walk on one of the streets in the center of the city. We were struck by the crowds walking on the sidewalks in two files, the ones going eastward walked on the outside and those going westward on the inside of the sidewalk. We quickly fell in line with one of the streams of walkers. The most pleasant experience of our visit to Dusseldorf was the visit to a park that had a large pond where beautiful, white swans were swimming about. One swan was followed by her young chicks-a picturesque, poignant scene.

We left Dusseldorf and flew to Zurich, Switzerland, which was charming, friendly and was bustling with tourists, many of them Americans. As we began to walk around the center we could see the majestic, snowcapped peaks of the Alps to the south. Lake Zurich on whose northern tip the city is located provided another breathtaking view with its lakeside promenades and the elegant homes. Another notable feature was the cleanliness of the streets, crowded by pedestrians and with the trams going in different directions. What surprised us again was the large number of people who spoke English and I don't mean just the tourists. From the streetcar conductors to the store clerks and grocery vendors, the Swiss spoke English. We did some shopping, buying gifts for the relatives in Greece and souvenirs for us. The one thing I thought would be an excellent buy was a self-winding Omega gold watch. It was beautiful and it quickly replaced my first watch that my Aunt Bettie bought me for the first birthday that I celebrated in the USA, in January 1948, a stainless steel Movado.

On the second day of our visit to Zurich we took a train to Constance, Germany. Our short visit there was capped by a significant purchase. We entered a camera shop and we bought a Contaflex camera with telephoto lens, which came in the form of a half a binocular. We used this camera extensively while visiting Greece.

We left Zurich bound for Athens. The flight was less than three hours long and as the plane approached the western coast of Greece I could sense the excitement of seeing my native land again after 12 long years when my life had changed so much. The aerial view was moving. I was gripped by a mixture of pride, curiosity and expectation. The voice of the pilot came on to inform us that we would be flying over the city and that the Acropolis could be seen on the left side of the plane. Many of the passengers began to get up from their seats and move to the opposite side to get a glimpse of the city and the imposing Acropolis. We were sitting on the left side and I had a window seat. The view was majestic and exciting to see. The Acropolis came in plain view with the Parthenon crowning the top of the hill. Jane and I were at awe for the few minutes the plane took to cross over the city of Athens.

It was early afternoon when we arrived at our hotel. We immediately called our relatives, Uncles Niko Spyrou and Thanasos, my mother's brother, who lived in Athens; they would be our hosts. The next call was to Thessaloniki to talk to my parents.

We spent three days touring Athens and visiting with Uncle Nick and Uncle Thanasos, his wife, Aunt Lesvia, and their daughter Nitsa, who was now a grown up lady of 22 and a student at the University of Athens. We enjoyed visiting the museums, the Acropolis and the lively district of Plaka, with its narrow streets running uphill towards the Acropolis and the many taverns and restaurants, that welcomed the visitors with the aromas of grilled shish kabob, lamb chops and fish.

My eagerness to visit Thessaloniki was rapidly turning into an ardent desire and I recall feeling elated when we began our flight out of Athens. Once we arrived we went directly to my parents' new apartment in a high-rise building near the center of the city. We took the elevator to the sixth floor. The door to the apartment was open and there stood my mother; with arms outstretched she took me in her embrace and kissed me repeatedly. My father, just behind her, was equally moved as he hugged and kissed me. Jane was received with the same excitement and warmth. As we entered the apartment we were greeted by a large contingent of relatives who eagerly embraced and kissed us.

We managed to find a few free minutes to sit down and rest. Soon, however, people began asking questions about life in Peru, my directing the project on burn patients and my plans for the future. What impressed my family the most, was that the US Government entrusted me with the responsibility of running the research project. Although Uncle Elias posed logical questions about the project, neither he nor the rest of the relatives had any concept of the medical and physiological issues faced by the burn research team, except Aunt Stasa, who was a dentist and had knowledge of vascular collapse and shock. My explanations of the significance of the project, the success of the treatment, the reasons for the large number of burn cases among the poor and indigent population captivated my relatives. The pride was even more evident with my father and mother who saw in me an accomplished individual who ten years after leaving Greece to emigrate to the U.S. was in a position to be entrusted by the U.S Government to direct a very important medical and social project in a foreign land, with a different language and unique social customs. The adulation ended early in the evening and then both Jane and I, overly tired from the trip, retired to our bedroom.

During the next few days we spent our time visiting the various relatives in their homes, where we feasted on tasty dinners of Greek cuisine. Aunt Zografia and Uncle Stavros went out of their way to show us their culinary talents. We made almost daily visits to see Aunt Helen, Uncle Minas and above all, my Yiayia, (grandmother), Evdoxia, who at this time was 87 years old. She went on to live another 14 years, dying at 101. Aunt Helen had a beautiful penthouse apartment on the seventh floor of a high-rise building that faced east and provided a fantastic and a breathtaking view of the Aegean, the White Tower, the park, the eastern part of the city and the mountain of Hortiatis in the background. From her balcony we were treated to views of magnificent sunrises and at night the light of the silvery full moon.

The trip back to visit Thessaloniki fulfilled another long held desire, to be reunited with my high school classmates. These were the friends with whom I spent seven years in the same classrooms, the boys with whom I began to interact with as an eleven year old boy and grew up with into my teen-age years. Our lives and adolescences passed through the carefree, pre-war period and into the catastrophic period of German occupation, with starvation, persecutions, and executions. These were the young men who had fought with me in the resistance and then together shared the joy and delirium of the days after the liberation. While some had moved abroad after the war, there were several classmates who remained in Thessaloniki after their university studies. There were many notable accomplishments. George Kostopoulos, who inherited his father's medical clinic and in time built a new one adjacent to the old. Another friend, Nasos Michalopoulos, graduated from the University of Thessaloniki with a degree in mathematics and then attended the Polytechnic University of Athens, where he received a degree in civil engineering. Alekos Marketos graduated from the University of Thessaloniki with a degree in mathematics, which allowed him to teach high school math. He eventually became a superintendent of schools. Yiannis Assimis also received his degree in mathematics and became a high school math teacher and then also a superintendent of schools. Mimis Kazakides, a talented classical violinist, received his medical degree and specialized in microbiology. George Gratsanis entered his father's business and when his father retired, he took over the management of the typography shop. Sotiris Tjiridis went into civil service and worked in the customs office of the Port of Thessaloniki. Nikos Triantafillou became a lawyer and lived in Athens.

The class reunion that we organized in Thessaloniki was represented by a small group of these former classmates. Those present were Kostopoulos, Kazakides, Gratsanis, Dimitriadis, Socotis and Mustakas; the latter two from the classes of prewar years but still part of our group of friends. Some were married and brought their wives. I treated everyone to a colored slide show with scenes from Chicago, Lima, and other cities from Peru including Huancayo, Cuzco, Machu Picchu and Piura. The pictures from Peru generated many questions and a great deal of discussion. Everyone was fascinated with the natives in Huancayo and Cuzco. Women dressed in colorful costumes and each one wearing a traditional hat, a custom that was probably imported from Europe.

The time in Thessaloniki was taken up by more visits to some of the suburbs and towns near the city. We also decided to visit the island of Rhodes with my parents. We flew to Athens and then took an overnight boat trip to Rhodes. Daybreak came as the boat was entering the harbor of the city of Rhodes. At the entrance, two massive columns, with an elk on top of each, adorned the passage into the harbor. It was there that the Colossus of Rhodes, a gigantic bronze statue, stood as the ancient ships sailed underneath it.

The city of Rhodes with its abundant palm trees, stone paved streets, buildings of varied architecture and design, bears many emblematic marks of the various conquerors and their cultures that passed through the island in the course of time. The old city is full of tourist shops, cafes, restaurants and museums.

After the ancient Greeks, came the Romans and they, like the people who came after them, left their mark. The most impressive structures that we admired were the medieval walls and towers that once protected the city under the aegis of the Knights of Rhodes.

At one end of the town we discovered a very old synagogue and a lady who was looking after it. I remember greeting her and asking if she knew how many of the 1,700 deported Jewish citizens of Rhodes ever returned to the island after the end of World War II, but she could not give us any numbers. If any survived, the number must have been very small. For comparison, out of the 44,000 Jewish people deported from Thessaloniki by the Nazis,, only about 1,000 made it back home.

My parents enjoyed Rhodes. They were enthralled at the variety of things they saw and were surprised to discover people living in the old town who were Turks and whose families had been there from before the fall of the Ottoman Empire during the First World War. Some of the Turkish families decided to remain in Rhodes following the exchange of populations between Greece and Turkey in 1922. Both my parents, who were fluent in Turkish, enjoyed talking to the Muslims they encountered.

On the second day of our stay in Rhodes we visited the New Town, which lies outside the walls of the Old City. New Town was created by Greek inhabitants who stayed on the island and chose not to follow the Knights in 1522 when the Ottomans invaded. Today this section of Rhodes is a true modern city. In 1912, Italy annexed Rhodes along with the other Dodecanese Islands. The Italians built new structures, several art deco buildings and new high-rise apartments. A number of the municipal buildings erected by the Italians bear the influence of

Arabic architecture. The streets are paved and are kept clean. My parents were particularly joyful since this was for them the first long vacation in many years.

The Acropolis at Lindos, with its Temple of Athena, is older than the one in Athens but it doesn't exactly match the grandeur of the latter. The top of the hill was adorned with columns, remnants of the ancient temple and of other unknown structures. Before we returned to the city of Rhodes, we lingered a little longer to admire the beautiful sunset as the sun painted the sky with fiery colors.

The last site that we visited was an unexpected surprise. We visited the valley of the butterflies. We were instructed to proceed to a cave, where myriads of butterflies nested. As we stood inside the cave by the entrance, we could easily observe what appeared to be thousands of little creatures, with colorful wings, plastered against the walls in layers, one on top of another. We were told that clapping our hands would stir the butterflies and they would begin to fly, and so they did! (Now, clapping is forbidden as research has revealed that this noise disturbs the insects' metabolic balance.) When they flew, the swarm of butterflies was a rare and awesome sight.

On the fifth day of our trip we took the ferryboat to Piraeus, the port of Athens, then back to the city where my parents took the plane to Thessaloniki. After my parents left Athens, Jane and I traveled to southern Peloponnesos to visit her parent's relatives in the town of Filiatra. There, we met her maternal grandmother, her mother's brothers and their wives and her cousins. We spent our time visiting the homes of each of the relatives and we were treated to wonderful Greek cuisine. We had an afternoon picnic by the sea and the cousins got together and sang and danced to the tunes of popular Greek songs that one of Jane's cousins, Koulis, played on his guitar.

After about five days in Filiatra we returned to Athens to prepare for our return trip to the USA and Peru. However, before the long trip back to South America, we visited Rome for a few days. The visit to Rome was particularly memorable and fortuitous.. We were lucky to be hosted by Sister Sophia, a nun of the Carmelite Order and a niece of the Mother Superior of the same order that ran the Children's Hospital in Lima, the headquarters for the burn project. Sister Sophia, who had been informed of our impending arrival, contacted us at the hotel where we were staying. The day after our arrival she came in her chauffer-driven car and took us around to some of the main sights of the city. She was extremely accommodating and eager to please us. Since she was originally from Spain, we conversed always in her native tongue. We were shown several ancient Roman structures as well as modern edifices. Architecturally, the old and the new worlds appeared at times incongruous and at times comfortable and balanced with each other. We visited St. Peter's Square and the adjacent Cathedral. Inside the church proper we were struck by the richness of the interior architecture, the many paintings by Italian masters and the statuary representing the work of renaissance artists. The *piece de resistance* was of course the Pieta, by Michelangelo. The beauty, the poignancy, the sadness and the grief of the moment were all captured in the faces and bodies of Christ and the woman supporting him, the virgin Mary, his mother.

The second day of our visit with Sister Sophia was again full of interesting surprises. We were fortunate to be in the square facing the balcony from which the Pope blesses the crowds. Sister Sophia was visibly excited when the Pope appeared on the balcony and began his blessings. There were several other nuns and priests among the throngs of lay people, many of them tourists like us. Our final visit with Sister Sophia was the Sistine Chapel with its unbelievable and incomparable painted mural ceiling. Even though the paintings were high above us, we could not help but be moved by the enormity of the powerful bodies; I recall them as anything but saintly, as they loomed with determination in the process of creation.

At the end of the day, we bid good-bye to Sister Sophia and we thanked her profusely for giving us such a wonderful time and experience. On the fifth day after our arrival we took the TWA flight back to Washington, DC and then on to Lima.

On our arrival in Lima, we were greeted by our friends from the hospital, including Drs. Augusto Bazan, Manuel Bocanegra, and Peter Stastny as well as our chief clinical technician, Dorita.

The following day I hosted the project physicians and staff to a slide show of the sites we visited in Europe and especially in Greece.

*In research, the horizon recedes as we advance
and is no nearer at sixty than it was at twenty.*
Marc Pattison, *Isaac Casaubon, 1875.*

CHAPTER 9

Evaluating The Project Data
At The End Of Three Years

OUR RETURN TO LIMA from Europe marked the beginning of my third year with the burn project. During our absence, additional cases were admitted and were handled ably by the staff. Dr. Augusto Bazan was tirelessly working to find ways for the local treatment of the wounds in the burned children and to create conditions favorable for skin grafting, his specialty skill. His dedication was exemplary and his devotion to the welfare of the patients unparalleled. It was always extremely gratifying to see a child survive severe burns and hospitalization and return to his or her family with the skin grafts in place and sometimes only minor disfigurement. Everyone among the medical and technical staff was working diligently, trying their best to make the project a success. Dr. Manuel Bocanegra, the chief clinical doctor, was on call 24 hours a day. He, with the aid of Dr. Napoleon Hinostrosa, would make the initial assessment of the patient's condition and assign him or her to the appropriate treatment regimen. Dr. Jose Antonio Arana, an excellent microbiologist, with the aid of his dedicated assistant Loli, took appropriate cultures on admission from all burn cases. Blood cultures were taken also on the second and third day after admission and whenever was indicated thereafter, to establish the earliest time of development of septicemia. The appearance of some positive blood cultures on admission and on the second or third day, suggested that the shock may have been facilitated by an early bacteremia.

As the third year of clinical research and data acquisition progressed, we began to analyze our findings in preparation for publication. By the summer of 1960 we had accumulated data from 454 burned patients who were admitted with burns involving 10 to 90% of body surface area. The likelihood of death from shock in 133 severely burned children treated with saline or saline in combination with albumin was 15 percent. The chance of the patient dying was not helped by the addition of albumin. Saline solution alone was just as effective as the two treatments given together. But in 321 alternate cases that were directed into other treatment arms to test other combinations, we found unique successful treatments. In those treated either with saline solution alone or plasma alone, saline solution in combination with plasma and gamma globulin or saline solution combined with albumin and gamma globulin, a significant decrease in shock mortality occurred. We believed this effect illustrated the role of infection in the early mortality of burned children and demonstrated the benefit conferred by gamma globulin. Infection seemed to be the key factor leading to mortality in these patients; we observed positive blood cultures or infected skin lesions in a high percentage of the patients who died between twenty-four and ninety-six hours after injury.

In burns involving 10 to 30 per cent of body surface area, plasma administered for shock therapy, or large intramuscular doses of gamma globulin, reduced delayed mortality by approximately 50% compared mortality of patients who received only saline solution or saline solution in combination with albumin. This reduction in mortality was observed in children under six; beyond this age, the early and late mortality was quite low in all therapy groups. The reduction in delayed mortality from the use of plasma or gamma globulin or both was due primarily to a decrease in the incidence of septicemia caused chiefly by *Pseudomonas aeruginosa*.

In children with burns covering 31 to 90 percent of body surface area, plasma or gamma-globulin therapy reduced shock mortality, but the majority of the children surviving shock died at a later interval from septicemia.

The results made a strong case for saline solution in combination with plasma as the preferred treatment for severe burns in young children. We concluded that the use of albumin, plasma expanders or saline solutions alone should be restricted to emergency conditions, and when used, these agents should be fortified by larger doses of gamma globulin given intramuscularly. Today, pooled human gamma globulin has been replaced by microorganism specific hyper-immune globulin.

These effects have not been observed in adults, in whom the acute and delayed mortality has been lower, with no difference between alternate groups treated with saline solution alone or in combination with plasma.

A report of these findings was presented at the First International Congress on Burns, in Washington, D.C., on September 19, 1960. The complete manuscript, with me as the first, and Dr. Rosenthal as the senior author, was published as the lead article in the New England Journal of Medicine on August 16, 1962, (New Eng. J. Med., 267: 317-323, 1962).

These studies clearly demonstrated that in an emergency situation where plasma is not available or where the number of casualties are so large that supplies of blood or plasma are inadequate, the use of saline solution is warranted to prevent shock from developing. The use of saline replacement therapy was instituted successfully several years after the findings of our burn project were published, during an epidemic of cholera in Southeast Asia, with enormous success. As is well known, patients with cholera develop massive diarrhea causing excessive loss of water and salt, which reduces the circulating vascular blood volume leading to irreversible shock.

As the time was rolling on in the early months of 1960, Jane and I were making plans for our return to Chicago. Dr. Rosenthal decided to come to Lima to assume the directorship of the project. He was approaching the retirement age of 65 and the two years he intended to spend with Mrs. Rosenthal in Lima served for him as a pre-retirement sabbatical. After all, the burn project was his idea. The enormous time and effort he invested in the animal experiments, which led to the clinical trials of the Peru burn project, did not receive the appropriate recognition within the scientific community. Dr. Rosenthal deserved a period of work under relaxed conditions in the project he created.

June 1960 – our last month in Lima, was taken up by endless invitations to dinners and farewell parties by friends and by the hospital staff. The truth is that we had made many good friends within the American community and among the Peruvian physicians and staff. Dr. and Mrs. Rosenthal arrived early in the month and moved into an elegant house in Miraflores, one of the exclusive suburbs of Lima. They gave a housewarming party, which served also as another farewell party for us.

We planned to leave Lima on a Boeing 707 jetliner one week before I was to begin my residency at the University of Illinois Research and Educational Hospitals. The farewell scene at the Limatambo Airport was emotional; many of the hospital physicians and personnel, including Dr. Rosenthal, came to wish us bon voyage. There were many *fuerte abrazos*, strong embraces, and wishes for us to return soon to Lima. Our first trip on a jet plane was an unequaled, almost exhilarating experience. The high speed and the relative quietness gave us a sense of awe.

We arrived next in Miami, where we took a connecting flight to Chicago. We proceeded immediately to the Staff Apartments on the University of Illinois Campus, the same building we occupied for almost five years before going to Peru. The next day I contacted the Department of Medicine where I was to begin my residency training in Internal Medicine on July 1, 1960.

Fig. 12. In my second year as medical student, University of Illinois College of Medicine, Chicago, Illinois. The staff apartments in the background. 1953.

Fig. 13. A group of my third year classmates. University of Illinois College of Medicine. 1954.

Fig.14. Medical school graduation dinner with Dr. Richard Winzler, chairman of Biochemistry, front left. Jane to his left, I am next to Jane and Mrs. Jana Winzler, to my left. Other faculty members. June 1956.

Fig. 15. Children's Hospital, Lima, Peru. I am second from the right. Dr. Gilberto Morey, director of the hospital, next to me. Other hospital staff. 1958.

Fig. 16. Children's Hospital, Burn Project Research Lab. I am sitting and Dr. Ipolito Cruz, a pediatrician, is standing next to me. 1959.

Fig. 17. Christmas Party. Burn Project Research Lab. Dr. Kiko Arana, in the middle, Dr. Pedro Stastny, to the left and behind him is Dr. Ipolito Cruz. Dr. Nicolas Velarde, with moustache, in the back. 1959.

Fig. 18. Children's Hospital. Dr. Sanford M. Rosenthal, of NIH, initiator of the Burn Project, on the right. Dr. Antonia Ciudad, a pediatrician, in the middle and Dr. Augusto Bazan, the plastic surgeon. 1960.

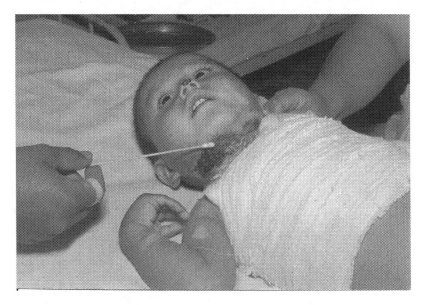

Fig. 19. Children's Hospital. Taking a skin culture from a burn patient. 1958.

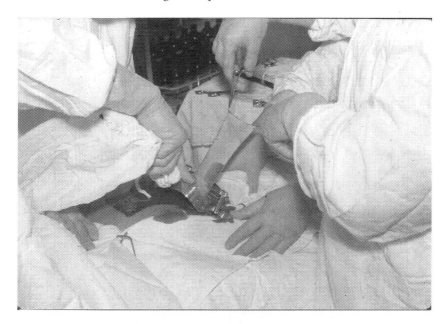

Fig. 20. Children's Hospital. Dr. Bazan, preparing a skin graft on the previous patient, (see fig. 19). 1958.

Fig. 21. Jane in front of our apartment building, San Isidro. Lima, 1959.

Fig. 22. Machu Picchu, the lost city of the Incas. Peru, 1959.

Fig. 23. The market at Huancayo, Peru, at 17,000 feet. Dr. and
Mrs. Mortensen on the right. Jane is on the left. 1958.

Fig. 24. Baby Llama, Cuzco, Peru, 1959.

Fig. 25.University of Illinois College of Medicine, Chicago,
Illinois. Graduation day. Conferring my Ph.D. degree.
My parents between Jane and me. June,1965.

Fig. 26. In front of our house, in Oak Park Illinois. My brother Chris on the right, his wife Rita on the left, Jane in the middle. Sandy, our oldest, in front of Chris, Patty in front of Rita and Paul, in Jane's arms. 1969.

Genius will live and thrive without training, but it does not the less reward the watering pot and pruning knife.
Diary from Thomas Wentworth Higginson,
Life of Margaret Fuller Osoli, 1884

—— CHAPTER 10 ——

Post-Graduate Training

ON THE FIRST DAY of my duties as a resident I was assigned to a number of patients and to two interns for whom I was responsible. Several members of the old nursing staff who were still working at the hospital were genuinely glad to see me back. It was reassuring to be in a pleasant, friendly environment where everyone was eager to help and make me feel at home. My initial concerns about how the senior faculty might react towards my not coming back after the second year were allayed when they received me with sincere expressions of friendliness and curiosity about my experiences in Lima. After all, it was their coaxing that made me accept the position at NIH and the directorship of the project.

The ensuing two years were full of intensive training with taking care of patients whose diseases varied from cardiac, to gastrointestinal, to infectious, to pulmonary, to hematologic, to liver, to kidney, to cancer problems. At that time the internal medicine service was one large unit without separate subspecialty divisions. However, the opportunity to train in an internal medicine subspecialty was there. Consultations were encouraged and we could ask for opinions of our colleagues not only from within our department of internal medicine but from other departments as well, such as surgery, neurology, radiology, urology, dermatology, ophthalmology or otorhino-laryngology.

There were several subspecialty conferences, grand rounds and journal clubs. It was said then, that the best informed physicians were the second year internal medicine residents and I believe it is likely still true to this day. At that point in our training, we were urged to read the major subspecialty journals as well as the general medicine ones, such as the New England Journal of Medicine, the American Journal of Medicine, the Lancet, the Archives of Internal Medicine, The Journal of Clinical Investigation and the Annals of Internal Medicine. At the end of the second year we were given our certificates and we were headed for various centers where we would train in a subspecialty of internal medicine. I chose infectious diseases since this was the area I had the most experience in after the years I spent following my internship working on the Peruvian burn project. I was appointed chief of the fellow trainees in infectious diseases at the Research and Educational Hospitals.

A few days into the fellowship, Drs. Harry Dowling, chief of medicine and Mark Lepper, my faculty advisor, asked me to meet with them. They indicated that the NIH Training Grant for the infectious diseases fellows provided funds for an advanced degree (in my case a Ph.D.) that was used to increase the salary stipend for the fellow as well as his lab expenses. They suggested that it would be an excellent opportunity for me and that, since I had my Master of Science in biochemistry, the course work was not going to be very heavy. I was taken by surprise at the suggestion and found myself at a loss as to how I should respond. Here I was, a fellow and chief of the fellows in infectious diseases and a junior attending physician at Cook County Hospital, asked to also become a graduate student. I felt overwhelmed by responsibilities already and

I wondereed what was going through my professors' minds. The time and effort I was expected to devote successfully to all these duties was extraordinary. Subsequently, I learned that if the fellowship program produced two or three Ph.D. fellows it would reflect very well on my superiors and a renewal grant application.

Having considered the advantages and disadvantages of my pursuing the Ph.D. program, I decided to accept the challenge. Several factors motivated me. In those days I was still moved by deferential and reverential feelings towards my professors. At the same time I had easily convinced myself that I would be capable of carrying on all those responsibilities. Finally, it was pointed out to me that the Ph.D. program provided for a significantly higher annual stipend, something close to $9,500 per year—that would really improve our standard of living. As a resident I was getting $1,800 per year and as a fellow the stipend was only slightly higher —$3,600 per year.

My clinical mentor, Dr. Mark Lepper, who was chairman of Preventive Medicine, discussed the nature of the research topic that he recommended I work on. My thesis advisor was to be Dr. Richard Winzler, chairman of Biochemistry. He wanted me to study the kidney and characterize the protein composition of the well known membranes—the basement membranes—in the functional unit of the kidney—the glomerulus. The main function of the membrane was to filter all of the blood flowed as the kidney produces urine. The decision to focus on this structural question in the kidney was based on the fact that several immunohistochemical and ultramicroscopic studies in patients with post-streptococcal glomerulonephritis (a serious form of kidney injury following common infection) or nephrotic syndrome (one of the most common causes of kidney failure in diabetic patients) demonstrated thickening of the kidney glomerular basement membrane as well as deposits of the patient's immunoglobulins on the membrane. Dr. Lepper gave me a tall order, "Find out what the antigenic components of the glomerular basement membranes are." He wanted me to identify the parts of the glomerulus that were the molecular targets of the body's immune system in these conditions. Except for amino acid and carbohydrate analyses, which suggested the presence of proteins and carbohydrates, we knew next to nothing of the number and nature of the specific protein or proteins in the basement membrane. The presence of hydroxyproline made people think of collagen and the presence of glucose, galactose and sialic acid suggested the presence of glycoproteins—proteins that were linked to sugars. My task of preparing adequate amounts of glomerular basement membrane was facilitated by Dr. Cecil Krakower's technique for isolating glomeruli from the kidney cortex, separating them from contaminating fragments of kidney tubules (another structural element in the kidney organ) and then disrupting the cellular components by sonication a process called "lysis"— that resulted in in cell-free, isolated basement membranes. This extraction process allowed me to focus on characterizing the glomerular basement membrane. The person who helped me with the technique and to whom I am immensely grateful, was Mr. Seymour Greenspan, the Chief Assistant in Dr. Krakower's laboratory.

The source of normal kidneys was autopsy cadaver material from the Department of Pathology at the University of Illinois. Dr. Krakower, who was chairman at the time, facilitated the procurement of kidneys. However, the need to have normal human kidneys and the departmental policy to allow removal of significant amounts of kidney material for histologic or other enzymatic studies, made it difficult to collect adequate amounts of normal, human kidney tissue for my studies. The problem was solved by changing from human to dog kidneys, which became available in significant numbers from experiments in the Department of Physiology. With adequate quantities of normal dog glomerular basement membrane at hand, supplemented by that from normal human kidneys, I proceeded to run a number of amino acid and carbohydrate analyses. Large quantities of hydroxyproline, hydroxylysine and glycine suggested the presence of a collagenous protein associated with high amounts of carbohydrates or of a collagen in association with one or more glycoproteins. The large amounts of cysteine as well as of lysine and hydroxylysine suggested in addition high degree of inter and intra molecular cross-linking. Later studies confirmed this.

The big task for me was to develop ways of solubilizing the basement membrane without destroying the structure of the individual protein components. Solubilization would make it easier separating and fractionating the different protein components. We first used 8-molar urea to obtain an initial phase of solubilization. This was followed by reduction and alkylation of disulfide bonds in the presence of 8 molar urea and we were pleased to see more complete solubilization.

Chromatographic analyses of soluble material showed fractions that were still composed of more than one protein component. To isolate the collagen from the other protein components we resorted to limited enzymatic digestion using different enzymes. This procedure solubilized the major portion of basement membranes, including that of the glomerulus, the Descemet's membrane and the lens capsule of the eye and gave us fractions that were characterized as collagenous, based on the glycine, hydroxyproline and hydroxylysine content. The protein we purified and we called basement membrane collagen had physical properties similar to those exhibited by the interstitial collagen (Type I).

In January 1966, I published a short paper in "Biochemical and Biophysical Research Communications" announcing the isolation of a collagen of unusual composition and a glycoprotein from glomerular basement membrane. This announcement was received with a very negative reaction by two labs; the collagen group at the NIH Institute of Dental Research that worked with Type I collagen. This group was headed by Dr. Karl Piez. And it was also greeted negatively by the lab of Dr. Robert Spiro at Harvard University. Spiro was a glycoprotein biochemist, interested in the biochemical changes of basement membranes in diabetes mellitus. Dr. Spiro had a personal interest in the biochemical changes in diabetes since he had been diagnosed with Type 1 diabetes at a younger age. Both research groups felt that I was intruding on their research domains and proclaiming new information that was at odds with the conventional wisdom. The first group of researchers, told the research community during national research meetings that there could not be another collagen besides Type I and the second lab group insisted that, a collagen associated with so much sugar, could not exist unless it was alternating with non-collagen glycosylated peptide sequences. They refused to acknowledge my work to the contrary, despite my scientific proof and publications in peer-reviewed journals. At this stage and for several years afterwards Dr. Spiro remained rather oblivious of the structural and biosynthetic properties of procollagen and collagen and could not accept the presence of a new collagen, a new gene product, that was named Type IV collagen.

One of the arguments promulgated by the NIH group was their dogmatic insistence that any new collagen had to conform to the physicochemical properties that had already been attributed to Type I collagen. They believed that the amino acid Glycine must comprise about 1/3 and the amino acid hydroxyproline about 10% of the residues and moreover they stressed that ultrastructurally the molecule must form fibrils with the typical 640 Angstrom spacing if it were to be considered a type of collagen. The collagen in basement membrane did not have a similar appearance by electron microscopy either on transmission electron microscopy of tissue sections or on rotary shadowing electron microscopy in solution. One unique property of interstitial collagen molecules is their ability to form SLS (Segment Long Spacing) aggregates in the presence of ATP, as revealed by electron microscopy. However, after limited treatment of the glomerular basement membrane with pepsin, such aggregates were obtained with the collagen of basement membrane. We accomplished the same effect with extracts of weak acetic acid from the lens capsule. A paper we published in 1973 in the European Journal of Biochemistry with Bjorn Olsen, as the first author, and Robert

Alper and myself, clearly demonstrated ATP aggregates of lens capsule collagen, showing the non-collagenous domains at one end.

While all these studies were going on, Dr. Edward Miller, working at the NIH Institute of Dental Research, discovered interstitial collagens Type II, in 1973 and Type III, in 1974, thus eliminating the argument that Type I collagen held a monarchical place in the collagen field. Basement membrane collagen was suddenly accepted by the Type I collagen group as a *bona fide* new molecule in the collagen famiy.

In the meantime, Dr. Spiro continued his unrelenting attacks on the existence of a new collagen, dismissing it because of its unique molecular structure which included the persistence of the non-collagenous domain, after the molecule was secreted by the cell and deposited in the extracellular space.

Using immunochemical studies we were able to identify at least three major antigenic components in the glomerular basement membrane and the lens capsule. One of them was the collagen molecule and the others were two glycoproteins, one of large molecular weight and the other of small molecular weight. Subsequent studies in our laboratory and in those of others confirmed the presence of a distinct collagen, which I termed collagen type IV in 1973, some seven years after first describing its existence in 1966. In addition, other laboratories at NIH, in Bethesda and at the Max-Planck Institute, in Martinsried, Germany confirmed the presence of a large molecular weight glycoprotein, which was given the name "laminin." The smaller one was isolated by researchers at the University of Pittsburg, and was termed "entactin". Entactin is also known by a later name:"nidogen."

A tumor in mice grew with a matrix that contains all the components of basement membrane and this cell line provided the material for the isolation of collagen type IV and of laminin and entactin in their native form. These structures were revealed in detail by rotary-shadowing electron microscopy.

Interest in my work on basement membranes was beginning to

mount. In the fall of 1964 I was in the process of finalizing the writing of my Ph.D. thesis for its defense in the spring of 1965. In April of 1965, I was at a party, given by a colleague, Dr. Klaus Kutner, on the south side of Chicago. There, I met Dr. Martin Mathews, a renowned collagen biochemist, who wanted to know about my thesis work. When I finished telling him about the presence of a collagen-like protein in basement membrane found in association with two glycoproteins, he became quite curious and excited. He told me that the research group he worked with at the University of Chicago had weekly seminars and asked me whether I would be willing to present my work at one of them. The research group at the University of Chicago was headed by Dr. Albert Dorfman, a world-renowned, proteoglycan expert and chairman of Pediatrics at the University.

After the seminar, which was given at Dr. Mathews' home, we all gathered in the kitchen for coffee and doughnuts. Dr. Dorfman approached me and questioned me about my research and asked when I expected to finish writing my thesis. I explained that my plan was to graduate in June 1965. Suddenly and totally unexpectedly he asked me whether I would like to join his group as assistant professor in the Department of Medicine at the University of Chicago on the tenure tract with a laboratory at La Rabida Institute. Even though, at the time, I was an assistant professor at the Department of Medicine at the University of Illinois and I enjoyed my clinical responsibilities, my research was moving at a snail's pace because of lack of research support after the fellowship ended. As quickly as Dr. Dorfman came up with the offer, I didn't negotiate for any details and answered as quickly with a "yes."

Dr. Dorfman presented me with a wonderful opportunity to have a faculty appointment at one of the most prestigious universities in the United States and carry out my research in the midst of some of the leading investigators in the connective tissue. Dr. Dorfman's group included leaders like Martin Mathews in the field of collagen research, Dr. Anthony Cifonelli in proteoglycan research and Dr. Dorfman himself in the area of heritable disorders of connective tissues, especially genetically mediated proteoglycan disorders. This was one of the best opportunities of my professional career. Although I had made major strides in identifying the major macromolecular components of basement membranes, I was still faced with many unanswered questions, such as the intracellular parhway of biosynthesis of the protein components in basement membranes and the presence of proteoglycans in the composition of the membranes. Initial studies in our lab at La Rabida led to believe that the very small amount of proteoglyacan found was a contaminant. We were proven wrong some 12 years later when Drs. Marilyn Farquhar and Yashpal Kanwar demonstrated the presence of proteoglycans as integral components of glomerular basement membranes.

Questions of how the various structural components of type IV collagen were synthesized in the body and their structural organization, ultrastructural morphology and their amino acid sequence, also remained to be answered. After I moved to the University of Chicago, I was given a large laboratory and office space to carry out my work. Dr. Dorfman provided funds for two senior technicians and all the laboratory facilities and supplies I needed to answer questions of the molecular nature of the basement membranes.

My research moved at a fast pace and by 1968 I was promoted to associate professor of medicine with tenure. Although the biosynthesis of basement membranes and their components was of paramount importance, in the 1960's we had only two simple models to study biosynthesis: the cell-free system or the organ system. They both worked by following the incorporation of radiolabeled precursors into proteins or proteoglycans. The two major cell types on either side of the glomerular capillaries were the epithelial and endothelial cells, which had not yet been isolated and grown in culture. Using radioactive sulfate as a precursor in cell-free system of kidney glomeruli, we demonstrated that it could be incorporated into proteins. However, the system did not prove very practical since the radioactive counts incorporated into protein were very low.

The biosynthetic studies were put on hold until 1970 when I accepted a position at the University of Pennsylvania Department of Medicine. There I joined the research group of Dr. Darwin Prockop who was working on the biosynthesis of interstitial collagen (collagen Type I) using leg tendons from 17-day-old-unhatched chicks.

Our studies with eye lens capsules were aided by Dr. Michael Grant, a postdoctoral fellow from England, who had joined the research group the same time I did. In the two years after arriving in Philadelphia, we produced three seminal papers, demonstrating for the first time the physical properties of newly synthesized and secreted basement membrane collagen. In one of the papers we stated that there was a time-dependent conversion of a larger molecular form to a smaller species in a way analogous to what was previously observed with interstitial collagen (Type I). This observation, which was proven to be wrong a year later, exemplified the pressure we felt from the researchers in the interstitial collagen field to demonstrate the same pathway for basement membrane collagen (now designated Type IV) as was shown for Type I.

Electron microscopic studies in our laboratory with undegraded, solubilized lens capsule collagen demonstrated the presence of long filamentous structures having a globular end at one end. This finding suggested that Type IV collagen was secreted in the form of what is called procollagen and deposited as such in tissues. Later studies, using organ cultures of mouse parietal yolk sac, by Dr. Ron Minor and Dr. Chris Clark in my laboratory, supported this conclusion. In the middle 70's several labs both in the USA and Europe began to investigate the nature of the structural molecular components of basement membranes. The laboratories of Dr. George Martin at NIH in Bethesda and of Dr. Rupert Timpl at the Max-Planck Institute in Martinsried, carried out a series of elegant experiments that characterized the molecular structure of the glycoprotein laminin and of Type IV collagen. The momentum of the studies by the NIH and the Max-Planck Institute and those from our laboratories stimulated an unprecedented amount of work that culminated in the discoveries of the genes that control the synthesis of these components as well as of other proteins that are associated with the basement membranes. Once the genes were identified, the investigators began to look into the biochemical basis of a variety of diseases that involve basement membranes, such as Alport and Goodpasture syndromes.

Fig. 27. At Dr. Darwin Prockop's home, in Philadelphia, Pennsylvania. Jane, sitting on the right, Ellie Prockop, between Darwin and me. September, 1970.

Fig. 28. Lab party at our house. Dr. Robert Alper, in the center, and Dr. Joel Rosenbloom, with the goatee, on the left. 1975

Fig. 29. Our lab group, The Connective Tissue Research Section, at the Philadelphia General Hospital. I am wearing a blue jacket. Jane is in front of me. 1973.

Fig. 30. First sabbatical. University of Oxford, Oxford, England. Aunt Helen, who visited us from Greece, behind Patty and Paul. Jane on the right and Sandy on the left. December, 1977-1978.

Fig. 31. The family at our house, in Merion Station, Pennsylvania. Jane on the left, I on the right, with Patty, Paul and Sandy in front. July, 1980.

Fig. 32. Second sabbatical. University of Oxford, Oxford, England. In my lab, at the Dunn School of Pathology, studying the effect on human endothelial cell infection by herpes simplex virus, Type 1, on protein synthesis. 1984-1985.

Fig. 33. International Symposium on Basement Membranes. Mishima ,Japan. I am addressing the Congress. 1985.

Fig. 34. Sandy at our home recovering from the bone marrow
transplant she received because of chronic myelogenous leukemia.
She developed Graft versus Host Disease, a common complication of
allogeneic transplants. She died on December, 24, 1991, at age 27.

Every man, wherever he goes, is encompassed
by a cloud of comforting convictions, which
move with him like flies on a summer day.
Bertrand Russell, *Sceptical Essays*, 1928

CHAPTER 11

Moving To The University Of Pennsylvania

IN THE FALL OF 1967, Dr. Darwin Prockop offered to me a six month
sabbatical in his lab, at the University of Pennsylvania. Although,
I initially accepted, I was unable to fulfill my promise because Jane
developed uterine bleeding, which led to her undergoing a complete
hysterectomy. Two years later Dr. Prockop presented me with a job
offer, arranging for me to move to the University of Pennsylvania and
join his lab. I was happy to accept the offer because Dr. Prockop was an
established authority in connective tissue research and particularly in
collagen.

The university offered me an appointment as Associate Professor
of Medicine with tenure. I traveled to Philadelphia and met with the
Chairman of the Department of Medicine, Dr. Arnold Relman and with
the Chief of the Medical Service at the Philadelphia General Hospital

(PGH), Dr. Truman Schnabel, where my lab was going to be and where I would be carrying my clinical responsibilities. Both meetings were cordial and pleasant.

The move from Oak Park, Illinois to Philadelphia, Pennsylvania turned out to be more challenging than expected for Jane and me. Certainly moving our young family to Philadelphia proved more daunting than our earlier child-free move to Lima. In the afternoon of the day of our departure we visited our next-door neighbors to bid them goodbye and stay for a small farewell party in our honor. The appetizers were tasty and the drinks thirst quenching. As it was the last week in June, the Chicago weather was rather oppressive. I did not refuse the offer of a glass of scotch whiskey on the rocks, which in time relaxed me and eased my concerns for the upcoming, long journey. Our plan was to depart in the evening and spend the night somewhere in eastern Indiana.

We set off around 7:30 P.M. from Oak Park, Illinois, in two cars, our new 1970 Pontiac sedan with air conditioning and our two year old, Pontiac coupe which had no air conditioning.The cars were packed full with our three children, our portable belongings and our one and only cat, Susie. I was driving the new Pontiac with our oldest daughter, Alexandra (Sandy) in the passenger seat. Jane, Patricia (Patty), Paul and "Susie the Kitty" were in the older Pontiac following close behind. Patty and Paul had negotiated between themselves that they would alternate sitting in the passenger seat, with a switch each time we stopped for whatever reason.

We hadn't even left the city of Chicago when, Jane suddenly began honking and started pulling over into the parking lot of the Museum of Science and Industry. The first casualty of the moving voyage was Susie the Kitty, who was suffering from car sickness. Jane helped her out of the car to get some fresh air and after the cat felt better, Jane put her back in the car next to Paul, she nuzzled next to him and the trip continued.

The eastbound Interstate 80 was wide open and we were making good time—but for only a very short time— before I began to feel that I might fall asleep at the wheel. It was still early in the evening, but with all the excitement and the farewell scotch whisky our neighbors had served us before we left, my ability to stay alert was challenged. Although we hadn't traveled as far as we had wanted,I decided to get off at the next exit and look for a hotel for the night. No sooner did we get into our rooms we were sound asleep. We woke up the next morning refreshed and ready to go again.

We continued our trip eastward crossing the rest of Indiana and then Ohio and by evening we reached the Ohio-Pennsylvania border. We got off at the Youngstown exit and we spent the night at a Holiday Inn. The next day we crossed Pennsylvania and by early afternoon we were in the suburb of Radnor on the outskirts ofPhiladelphia. That put us about eight miles west of our destination on Meeting House Lane, in Merion Station, Pennsylvania, a suburb just two miles west of the Philadelphia city line. We checked into the Treadway Inn and the rest and relaxation were welcomed by every member of the family, including "Susie the Kitty".

The next morning, after breakfast, we returned to our rooms only to find out that the maid refused to make up one of the rooms because there was a "beast" lying under the bed. Although "wild" Susie had normal features as any feline through history, her first cross-country car trip had not put her in a very hospitable mood.

We packed up and were on the road again and by noon we were parked on the driveway of our new home, a beautiful southern colonial style house with four white columns on the front entrance and a side porch with similar but smaller columns.

Soon the van with our household effects from Oak Park arrived and the unloading and arrangement of the furniture began. That night we all slept on our beds for the first time since we had left Oak Park three days earlier. This was to be our new home and was to remain so to this day 42 years later.

Merion Station is one of several towns in Lower Merion Township, which borders Philadelphia. The neighborhood is characaterized by the lush green growth of several varieties of trees, evergreens, firs, elms, magnolias, ash, maple, white birch as well as several fruit trees, from apple to peach and quince. Our new home sat on a corner and facing south, so on sunny days the whole house is bathed in bright sunlight. We settled in to our new neigborhood as a family very quickly. The girls were enrolled in Cynwyd Elementary School, located very conveniently only two blocks from our home. Paul was too young for Cynwyd so he was enrolled in Harcum Junior College's preschool program.

On the first Monday after arriving in Merion Station, I began my work at the Philadelphia General Hospital (PGH), a sprawling medical center where the city's four medical schools shared the responsibilities of taking care of medical, surgical, pediatric and obstetrical patients. The Chief of the University of Pennsylvania Medical Service was Dr. Truman Schnabel, who answered to the moniker "Nipper". He was my superior in my clinical responsibilities. Dr. Schnabel was an excellent clinician with a caring attitude. He was a great role model to me and for the medical students and residents. He was always pleasant to talk to and eager to help with whatever needs presented at the time. My work day at PGH was divided between my hospital responsibilities and my research studies.

My research work was carried out in the extensive laboratory facilities of PGH, which were under the direction of Dr. Darwin Prockop. Dr. Prockop at the time was involved in studies which attempted to elucidate the intracellular steps in the biosynthesis of Type I collagen. My arrival at Dr. Prockop's lab coincided with the arrival of a post-doctoral fellow, Dr. Michael Grant, from Manchester University, in England.

Dr. Grant was to work under Dr. Prockop's and my supervision in the biosynthesis of basement membrane collagen, Type IV. He was a very bright and skillful investigator. He managed to isolate lenses from the eyes of 17-day-old chick embryos and used them to study the uptake of radioactive [C-14] proline in an *in vivo* and *in vitro* system, followed by the isolation of the [C-14] labeled extracellular proteins, where the presence of the major hydroxyproline containing fraction was identified after molecular fractionation. The studies with Michael Grant resulted in the publication of three seminal papers in the Journal of Biological Chemistry and established that the collagen synthesized by the lens capsule epithelial cells was a basement membrane collagen.

Dr. Charles Clark and Ron Minor, who joined my research group in the early 70's contributed significantly to the elucidation of the biosynthesis of basement membrane collagen in the rat parietal yolk-sac system. The latter studies were aided considerably by the technique of isolating the rat parietal yolk sac,developed by Drs. Robert Brent and Tom Kozalka of Thomas Jefferson University.

When I joined Dr. Prockop's laboratory in 1970, the research group put together a program project grant application to study biochemistry and metabolism of connective tissues. Program project grants were composed by separate, individual projects, having a common purpose. The grant was sent to NIH, and it was approved for five years for a total of $2,500.000. Dr.Prockop was the principal investigator (P.I.) and I was the Co-P.I. In 1972 Dr. Prockop decided to take a new job as Chairman of Biochemistry at Rutger's Medical School in New Jersey. I stayed at the University of Pennsylvania and became the P.I. of the program project and also the Director of the Clinical Research Center at Philadelphia General Hospital. Suddenly, I was in charge of a large research facility with large amounts of research funds and the ability to expand my research program. In 1975 the program project grant was approved for another five-year period. In the preceding years, several people had joined our research group, including Drs. Robert Alper, Charles Clark, Peter Dehm, Edward Macarak, Barbara and James Howard and Ron Minor. Our research on the structure and biosynthesis of basement membranes and basement membrane collagen (Type IV) was making notable strides.

MY FIRST SABBATICAL LEAVE

In 1976 I was reminded by the University administration that I was eligible for a sabbatical leave which was an opportunity to study and conduct research in another institution. For professors on sabbatical, the University offered either full salary for a six-month leave or 50 percent salary support for a full year away. I opted for half-support for the full year and to make up for the second 50 percent of my salary. I applied for a fellowship from the prestigious John Guggenheim Foundation. The fellowship was approved in March 1977 for 12 months and in September of that year I traveled to Oxford, England. I had made prior arrangements with Dr. Henry Harris, Director of the Dunn School of Pathology at Oxford University, to do my research at the Dunn School where many experts on genetics and cytogenetics were actively working. Dr. Harris was a world authority on cell fusion and my plan was to use cell fusion to locate the chromosome that held the gene responsible for the synthesis of Type IV collagen. Human endothelial cells, which synthesize and secrete Type IV collagen, were to be fused with mouse fibroblasts

The standard laboratory procedure that we used for inducing cell hybrids in *vitro* involved the addition of inactive Sendai virus to a culture containing two different cell types. In my case, we used mouse fibroblasts and human endothelial cells. Using this procedure, two groups of multinucleated cells are generated. The first group contained nuclei from only one parental type (homokaryons), while the second group contained nuclei from both parental types (heterokaryons). The latter group are considered hybrid cells. After subculturing, the heterokaryon may die, or it may survive and give rise to two mononucleated hybrid cells called synkaryons. As these hybrids continue to divide they gradually lose most of the chromosomes originating from one of the parental cells, in my case the human endothelial cells . The hybrid cells containing a small number and varied types of human chromosomes were subjected to chromosomal mapping analysis. Concomitantly, many of these hybrid cells were subjected to biochemical analysis to determine whether they produced Type IV collagen.

Working at the Dunn School was pleasant and scientifically rewarding. Everyone was more than helpful, from the Director, Dr. Harris to the research assistants and senior scientists to the administrative staff. To show my appreciation for their generosity and support of my project I was able to reciprocate by teaching several groups of researchers at the Dunn School and other Oxford University labs how to isolate and grow endothelial cells from human umbilical cord vein.

It was also exciting to be at The Dunn School of Pathology because of its special role in the history of science. The most notable contribution that came from The Dunn School was the work by Dr. Norman Heatley, demonstrating a method to isolate large quantities of penicillin that could be used in clinical trials of infected patients. The first patient to receive penicillin was a young boy who had developed cavernous sinus thrombosis secondary to streptococcal infection. The infection was cleared but the sinus thrombosis was so severe that the boy died. For their pioneering contribution the team of Sir Alexander Fleming, the discoverer of penicillin, Sir Ernst B. Chain, who worked out its chemical structure and Sir Howard W. Florey, the then-Director of the Dunn School and the principal investigator of the early clinical trials at Oxford, received the Nobel Prize in physiology or medicine in 1945. Unfortunately, Dr. Norman Heatley was left out of the honor, although it was his ingenuity to use ceramic containers to grow the fungus cultures in large volumes with high surface to volume ratios that were necessary for optimal antibiotic production.

At the time of my arrival at the Dunn School, Dr. Norman Heatley was still at work; my lab was next to his. He was very friendly and always willing to engage me in conversation about my project. His lab was full of small apparatuses that he himself built, at minimal cost to aid his experiments. He seemed fond of these many small machines and devices; his typewriter was one of the oldest models, a Royal.

In November 1977, Jane and the children arrived in Oxford. The children were immediately registered at the Bishop Kirk Middle School in Summertown, a beautiful suburb of Oxford. Our apartment was located in Summertown, on the second floor of a two-story house that had all the modernities that our American family was used to back home. It had three large bedrooms, a large kitchen, a good size laundry room, adequate closet space and two full bathrooms. The family that occupied the ground floor apartment was leaving England and we bought their Fiat sedan at a reasonable price of 2,200 pounds. Although it had a stick shift, both Jane and I struggled only a few days before we recalled our past training, driving stick shift cars.

In the Spring of 1978, Patty and I went to Paris, France. We spent a week visiting the sights, the large and small museums, the department stores, and promenaded on the wide boulevards and lush gardens. Patty was coming out of a devastating experience with anorexia nervosa. The visit to France with me as her only chaperone had a healthy and invigorating effect on her self-esteem and confidence. That same summer the whole family visited a beautiful resort place in Chalkidiki, Greece. The beaches of the Kassandra peninsula were beautiful and the children had an exceptionally memorable vacation. After these two excursions, Patty's problems with anorexia disappeared and thankfully never returned.

My stay at the Dunn School of Pathology was a valuable experience, which allowed me to learn new techniques and new concepts of cell biology. The cell fusion and the chromosomal mapping techniques that I practiced were very promising at the outset but ultimately they proved too problematic to be able to identify the exact chromosome responsible for the synthesis of Type IV collagen. In addition, the issues of chromosomal splitting and chromosomal translocations made definitive identification difficult. This goal had to wait another five years when gene cloning became available, which permitted the localization of the genes for $\alpha1$ and $\alpha2$ chains of Type IV collagen on chromosome 13.

In late July of 1978 we traveled back to the USA. We were amazed at the large number of personal and household effects that we had accumulated in less than a year. The five of us brought to the airport at Heathrow 26 pieces luggage, consisting of suitcases, packed boxes, carryon bags and the occasional extra sack. We easily exceeded our carry-on limits and were forced to check a number of flimsy bags with expensive clothing and gifts. When we arrived at JFK Airport we were surprised to find out that all our bags, boxes and paper shopping bags came through intact. We subsequently learned that one of the passengers on our plane was the late Princess Grace of Monaco. Two of my colleagues from the lab in Philadelphia, Drs. Chris Clark and Ed Macarak, had the good sense to rent a van, which accommodated all of us and our personal effects.

MY SECOND SABATICAL

In the fall of 1984 I took a second sabbatical, again at the Dunn School of Pathology of Oxford University. Jane and I were given an apartment in a complex owned by the University. Our children were older now, Sandy and Patty attending the University of Pennsylvania and Paul finishing Lower Merion high school. We accommodated ourselves in the new apartment, which had an extra bedroom for visiting children and relatives. The children visited us separately, during school holidays. Jane and I managed to travel throughout England either by bus or train.

It was during this year abroad that Uncle Elias paid us a visit at Oxford. Presently, he was living in Modena, Italy, with his adopted daughter Keti and her Italian husband, Salvatore. Uncle Elias spent a week in Oxford and availed to the easy accessibility of London to spend full days visiting the museums, the big department stores, the Symphony Hall and the numerous parks.

My research at the Dunn School of Pathology during my second sabbatical was centered on the effects of herpes simplex virus type 1 infection on the synthesis of extracellular proteins by human endothelial cells in culture. Using SDS-PAGE electrophoresis we observed that

[14C]-proline incorporation into fibronectin, type IV procollagen and thrombospondin was inhibited in infected cultures as early as 2 hours following infection, becoming almost complete by 15 hours post-infection. The degree of inhibition of matrix protein synthesis was dependent on the size of the virus inoculum - Multiplicity of Infection-20 (MOI-20) showed a greater effect than MOI 5 and progressed sequentially from one protein to the next; shut-off of type IV procollagen occurred first, followed by that of fibronectin and then throbospondin. Pulse-chase experiments suggested that the absence of labeled matrix protein in the medium of infected cultures is not due to accumulation of protein within the infected cells, since there was a parallel reduction of labeled protein in the cell layer, indicating an inhibition of actual protein synthesis.

In June 1985, I thanked Professor Harris and Dr. Michael Pfenick, in whose lab was working, and Jane and I returned home. The experience of learning how to grow viruses and use them in protein biosynthetic studies was very valuable for my future studies.

EPILOGUE

THE DECADE OF THE 90's began with a cruel, sad and devastating event. In February 1990, Sandy, our 26 year old daughter, told us that on a routine medical check-up for insurance she was told that her white count was greater than 30,000. She was promptly seen by a specialist from the hematology division of the University of Pennsylvania, and received the devastating diagnosis of chronic myelogenous leukemia, (CML).

I phoned professional contacts at the National Cancer Institute of the National Institutes of Health and they recommended that Sandy have a bone marrow transplant—saying that this would give the greatest chance for cure. The first hurdle was finding a suitable donor who possessed matching tissue types to permit a marrow transplant. Jane, Patty, then 24, and Paul 23 year olds and I were tested for matching histocompatibility antigens and compared to those of Sandy's and the verdict was that Patty was a "perfect match". The transplant, if it succeeded, could cure the cancer. Other, less aggressive therapies could slow the condition and might only stave off an inevitable decline. After weighing all the options, Sandy chose the courageous and proactive path and decided to go ahead with the bone marrow transplant. We looked at medical centers that had the most extensive experience with CML and the most aggressive treatments and chose the transplant center at the University of Minnesota in Minneapolis. Sandy, Jane and I visited the center and had a consultation where we learned more of the details of the transplant. After discussing the pros and cons and considering the rigorous and life threatening preparatory steps, like total body irradiation and systemic chemotherapy, it seemed that bone marrow transplant was the best choice and might give the greatest hope for a cure and long term survival. A date was set to begin the long treatment in September 1990. As a family, we made a temporary home in a hotel near the University of Minnesota Medical Center, so we could all support Sandy during this trial. The treatment protocol involved first completely ablating Sandy's immune sytem by destroying her bone marrow—the site of the cancer—using massive doses of toxic chemotherapy drugs and total body irradiation. Then the donor bone marrow specimen from Patty would be used to reconstitute Sandy's immune system. Sandy lost weight and weakened from the chemotherapy; she lost her hair and suffered painful side effects to her skin, mouth and throat. During the period before and after the transplant Jane lived day and night in the same room as Sandy, taking only time off to go to the hotel to bathe. Jane was totally dedicated to caring for Sandy and protecting her welfare during the long hospitalization.. In October 1990, Patty's bone marrow was given to Sandy and within a few days there was evidence that the transplant took.

Four weeks after the transplant, we all returned to Merion Station, our home. Initially things were going well and Sandy was followed by a doctor from the Hematology-Oncology Division of the University of Pennsylvania. However, by mid-December Sandy developed signs and symptoms consistent with graft versus host disease, better known by its acronym, GVH. Sandy's new immune cells, growing from Patty's donated marrow were attacking Sandy's tissues. This was not supposed to happen or should have been very rare in a case where the donor and recipient were perfectly matched. Sandy, Patty and I traveled to Minneapolis where Sandy was hospitalized and given immunosuppressive and anti-inflammatory agents. Jane and Paul later came to Minneapolis as well for what turned out to be another long hospitalization that stretched through the Christmas holidays and into the winter months of the new year. Valentine's Day would come before Sandy was home again. She was well enough to be at home but not yet back to normal and now felt changed both physically and emotionally by the illness and the intensive treatments meant to spare her life. She wept one day when a friend she ran into while shopping did not recognize her. There were many difficult days where she balanced medications and side effects, all the while continuing to hope and plan for a future for herself, a graduate degree, a career and a life with her fiancé. The family struggled with her and the days were alternately exhilarating, as we celebrated the promise of a cure or ponderous, when Sandy faced medical setbacks..

She returned to an independent life gradually in 1991 and moved in with her fiancé but as the year went on, she began to develop jaundice, which indicated liver involvement. In the end of 1991 her condition abruptly deteriorated as she weakened and experienced several infections related to her long term immunosuppression. As the Christmas holidays arrived, Sandy was hospitalized at the Hospital of the University of Pennsylvania. Late one night she had a seizure in the hospital and then gradually lapsed into coma. MRI of the brain revealed several brain abscesses and cultures established the presence of the fungus nocardia. She had fought for almost two years, but now faced a terminal complication

On December 24, 1991, Sandy died at the age of 27. Losing Sandy was emotionally devastating for our family. She had been full of vigor, and hope for life and her future. Seeing her grow up had given us so much pleasure. We miss her terribly and 20 years after her death, remembering her forms part of our daily existence.

As Sandy was battling an illness with an inexorable end, Patty and Paul entered medical school at the University of Pennsylvania in September 1991. They both did very well and in June 1995 they graduated. On the day of graduation I was given the opportunity to present the diplomas to both Patty and Paul. Patty pursued pediatrics for a year in Chicago and then switched to pathology. Paul took his internship and residency in internal medicine at the University of Chicago and specialized in gastroenterology.

The same month that Patty graduated, she also got married. The groom, Ted Theodosopoulos, is the son of a teenage friend of mine from Thessaloniki, Lakis Theodosopoulos. Lakis and I were part of the same resistance team during the German occupation. Ted attended the American School in Thessaloniki and then entered the Massachusetts Institute of Technology in Boston. He studied mathematics and received a BA, MS and a Ph.D. from the same institution.

Patty's wedding was a memorable event for our family but also for Ted's family, our relatives who came all the way from Greece, my cousins and Jane's cousins. Many of the guests were friends from the immediate geographic vicinity of Philadelphia and others from as far away as California, Chicago and other parts of the Midwest. California is where both my brother and currently Paul live and Chicago is where all the godparents of our children live. Jane's brother and his family arrived from western Illinois. We estimated that about 100 guests attended the wedding.

The wedding ceremony took place on May 5, 1965 at St. Luke's Greek Orthodox Church in Broomall, Pennsylvania, about 10 miles west of our home. The reception was held in our front yard under a massive tent. The mood of the guests and of the newlyweds was festive and complemented by a band specializing in Greek songs.

The catering company served an incomparable array of hors d'oeuvres and the main meals. At the end of the meal some people began to dance to the Greek music and the young people to the popular tunes of the time. The music was very loud and annoyed some people in the vicinity. The police arrived after some neighbors complained. We tried to tone down the music but were not too successful. It was well after midnight when the last of our guests left our house, well-satisfied with the food and the ambience of the evening.

In October 1996 Patty gave birth to a beautiful healthy girl that they named Alexandra. Two years later we baptized Alexandra in

Thessaloniki. The godmother was Eleni, the daughter of my cousin Doxa, daughter of my Aunt Helen.

Another memorable event of this decade was my retirement from the University of Pennsylvania on June 30, 1996 and assumption of the title "Professor of Medicine Emeritus". Since this was considered "early retirement", the contract allowed for continued salary for two more years with full health benefits. The last 15 years of retirement have remained busy and full of intellectual pursuits. I continued my research until the year 2002 when I closed my lab and I moved to the new building that the Science Center built to house the administrative offices of several of the biotechnology companies that moved to the new lab facilities. That same year I was appointed scientific mentor for more than 30 biotechnology companies at the Science Center. and I created a monthly lecture series at the Science Center that I dubbed "Lunch for Hungry Minds". The speakers were selected from the faculties of the universities in Philadelphia and the nearby University of Delaware, as well as from biotechnology companies residing at the Science Center or located in the southeastern Pennsylvania region. This lecture series has been a tremendous success for the past ten years.

In 1998 I was appointed Executive Chair of the Institutional Review Board (IRB) of the University of Pennsylvania, a position I held until 2002. These institutional committees review applications designed to carry out clinical trials involving human beings.

In 2002 a group of senior and emeritus faculty of the school of medicine formed the Association of Senior and Emeritus Faculty (ASEF). I was among its founding fathers along with my colleague at Penn in the Infectious Diseases Section, Dr. Rob Roy MacGregor. In 2010 I was elected president of ASEF and again in 2011 for a second term.

In March 2000, Patricia gave birth to a second beautiful little girl, Efthemia, named after Ted's mother, and in March 2002 she gave birth to a third child, a most attractive little girl, who was named Eugenia, which is Jane's given name. Both Efthemia and Eugenia were baptized in Thessaloniki, Greece.

All three of our granddaughters fill us with absolute joy and contentment as we march into our retirement years.